I0793955

Endorsements for the Flourish Bible Study Series

"The brilliant and beautiful mix of sound teaching, helpful charts, lists, sidebars, and appealing graphics—as well as insightful questions that get the reader into the text of Scripture—make these studies that women will want to invest time in and will look back on as time well spent."

Nancy Guthrie, Bible teacher; author, *Even Better than Eden*

"If you're looking for rich, accessible, and deeply biblical Bible studies, this series is for you! Lydia Brownback leads her readers through different books of the Bible, providing background information, maps, timelines, and questions that probe the text in order to glean understanding and application. She settles us deeply in the context of a book as she highlights God's unfolding plan of redemption and rescue. You will learn, you will delight in God's word, and you will love our good King Jesus even more."

Courtney Doctor, Coordinator of Women's Initiatives, The Gospel Coalition; author, *From Garden to Glory* and *Steadfast*

"My daughter and I love using Flourish Bible Studies for our morning devotions. Lydia Brownback's faithful probing of biblical texts; insightful questions; invitations to engage in personal applications using additional biblical texts and historical contexts; and commitment to upholding the whole counsel of God as it bears on living life as a godly woman have drawn us closer to the Lord and to his word. Brownback never sidesteps hard questions or hard providences, but neither does she appeal to discourses of victimhood or therapy, which are painfully common in the genre of women's Bible studies. I cannot recommend this series highly enough. My daughter and I look forward to working through this whole series together!"

Rosaria Butterfield, Former Professor of English, Syracuse University; author, *The Gospel Comes with a House Key*

"Lydia Brownback's Flourish Bible Study series has been a huge gift to the women's ministry in my local church. Many of our groups have gone through her studies in both the Old and New Testaments and have benefited greatly. The Flourish Bible Study series is now my go-to for a combination of rich Bible study, meaningful personal application, and practical group interaction. I recommend them whenever a partner in ministry asks me for quality women's Bible study resources. I'm so thankful Brownback continues to write them and share them with us!"

Jen Oshman, author, *Enough about Me* and *Cultural Counterfeits*; Women's Ministry Director, Redemption Parker, Colorado

"Lydia Brownback has a contagious love for the Bible. Not only is she fluent in the best of biblical scholarship in the last generation, but her writing is accessible to the simplest of readers. She has the rare ability of being clear without being reductionistic. I anticipate many women indeed will flourish through her trustworthy guidance in this series."

David Mathis, Senior Teacher and Executive Editor, desiringGod.org; Pastor, Cities Church, Saint Paul, Minnesota; author, *Habits of Grace*

"As a women's ministry leader, I am excited about the development of the Flourish Bible Study series, which will not only prayerfully equip women to increase in biblical literacy but also come alongside them to build a systematic and comprehensive framework to become lifelong students of the word of God. This series provides visually engaging studies with accessible content that will not only strengthen the believer but the church as well."

Karen Hodge, Coordinator of Women's Ministries, Presbyterian Church in America; coauthor, *Transformed*

"Lydia Brownback is an experienced Bible teacher who has dedicated her life to ministry roles that help women (and men) grow in Christ. With a wealth of biblical, historical, and theological content, her Flourish Bible Studies are ideal for groups and individuals that are serious about the in-depth study of the word of God."

Phil and Lisa Ryken, President, Wheaton College; and his wife, Lisa

"Lydia Brownback's Bible study series provides a faithful guide to book after book. You'll find rich insights into context and good questions to help you study and interpret the Bible. Page by page, the studies point you to respond to each passage and to love our great and gracious God. I will recommend the Flourish series for years to come for those looking for a wise, Christ-centered study that leads toward the goal of being transformed by the word."

Taylor Turkington, Bible teacher; Director, BibleEquipping.org

THE PSALMS OF ASCENTS

Flourish Bible Study Series
By Lydia Brownback

Judges: The Path from Chaos to Kingship

Esther: The Hidden Hand of God

Job: Trusting God When Suffering Comes

The Psalms of Ascents: Journey to Joy

Ecclesiastes: Finding Meaning When Life Feels Meaningless

Jonah: God's Relentless Grace

Habakkuk: Learning to Live by Faith

Luke: Good News of Great Joy

Romans: The Glory of the Gospel

Ephesians: Growing in Christ

Philippians: Living for Christ

Colossians: Fullness of Life in Christ

James: Walking in Wisdom

1–2 Peter: Living Hope in a Hard World

FLOURISH
BIBLE STUDY

THE PSALMS OF ASCENTS

JOURNEY TO JOY

LYDIA BROWNBACK

CROSSWAY®
WHEATON, ILLINOIS

The Psalms of Ascents: Journey to Joy

Published by Crossway
1300 Crescent Street
Wheaton, Illinois 60187

Cover design: Crystal Courtney

First printing 2025

Printed in China

All emphases in Scripture quotations have been added by the author.

Trade paperback ISBN: 978-1-4335-9031-3

Crossway is a publishing ministry of Good News Publishers.

RRDS 34 33 32 31 30 29 28 27 26
15 14 13 12 11 10 9 8 7 6 5 4 3 2

With gratitude to God
for
Erin Sullivan

Friend of my youth, beloved sister for eternity,
where I hope we will worship together on summer-bright sandy beaches.

CONTENTS

THE PLACE OF THE PSALMS OF ASCENTS IN BIBLICAL HISTORY

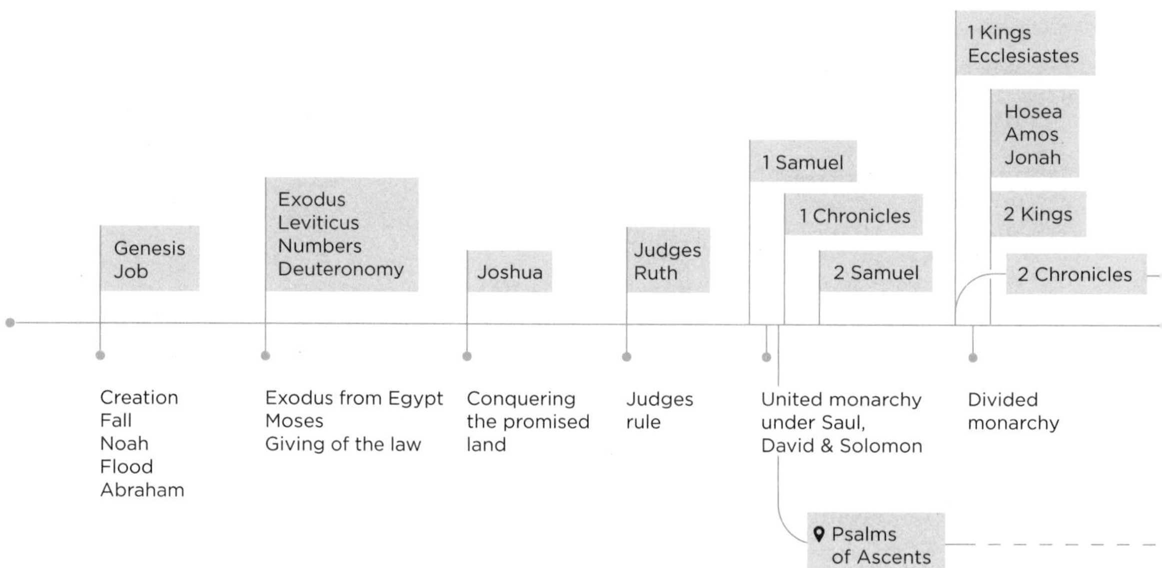

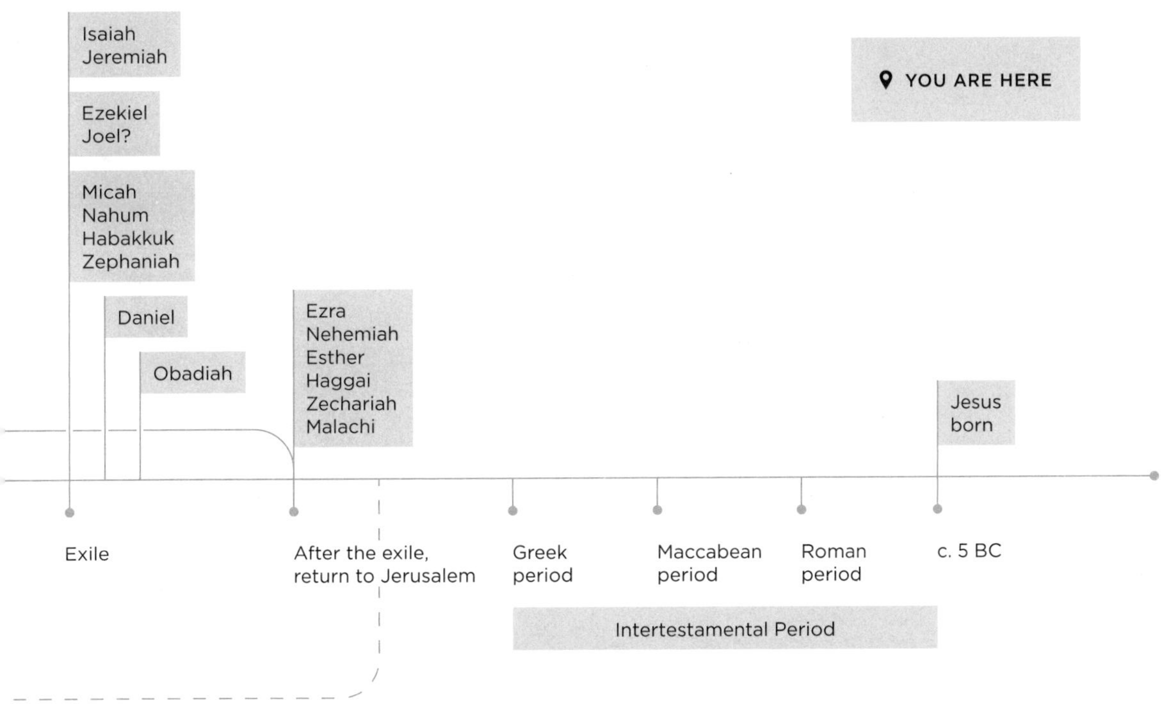
Isaiah
Jeremiah
Ezekiel
Joel?
Micah
Nahum
Habakkuk
Zephaniah
Daniel
Obadiah
Ezra
Nehemiah
Esther
Haggai
Zechariah
Malachi
YOU ARE HERE
Jesus born
Exile
After the exile, return to Jerusalem
Greek period
Maccabean period
Roman period
c. 5 BC
Intertestamental Period

INTRODUCTION

GETTING INTO THE PSALMS OF ASCENTS

A family roadtrip requires a good bit of advance planning. Loading up a cooler with snacks minimizes the number of stops for meals, and downloading entertaining videos keeps the kids from arguing. If your vehicle lacks high-tech amenities, tossing in some creative car games will help pass the long hours on the road. Getting ready to go is a significant undertaking. Imagine, then, the difficulty of traveling with a family hundreds of miles on foot. That's what families in ancient Israel did—and they did it three times a year! Old Testament law required God's people to journey from their homes to the city of Jerusalem to celebrate three annual festivals. They had no podcasts or videos to pass the hours, but they sang songs. Most Bible scholars believe that the songs they sang were the Psalms of Ascents, the focus of our study. Through these fifteen psalms, or songs, we enter into their experience—the weariness, the sin struggles, the hopes, and most of all the joy. Three times each year, they journeyed to joy. And the songs they sang along the way provide us with a blueprint for our own journey as disciples of the Lord Jesus Christ.

WHO'S WHO IN THE PSALMS OF ASCENTS

The traveling Israelites are in the background of each psalm we'll be studying. Four of these psalms are attributed to Israel's King David and one to his son Solomon. The author or authors of the remainder isn't known. The *what* is just as significant as the *who* when we study these psalms. The ark of the covenant, the most sacred fixture in Israel's worship, is a significant feature. The temple in Jerusalem, or Zion, plays a dominant role, not only as a destination to be reached but for what it symbolized to God's people.

SETTING

These fifteen psalms, Psalms 120–134, were composed at various times in Israel's history and were pulled together at some point into this collection, the Psalms of Ascents. As we've noted, it is assumed that as God's people traveled to Jerusalem for the annual worship festivals, they used the journey to reflect on God's faithfulness, offer praise and thanksgiving, and renew their commitment of faith and obedience. Three times a year they made the trek, according to God's instructions:

> Three times a year all your males shall appear before the LORD your God at the place that he will choose: at the Feast of Unleavened Bread, at the Feast of Weeks, and at the Feast of Booths. They shall not appear before the LORD empty-handed. (Deuteronomy 16:16)

Jerusalem in Its Heyday under King Solomon[1]

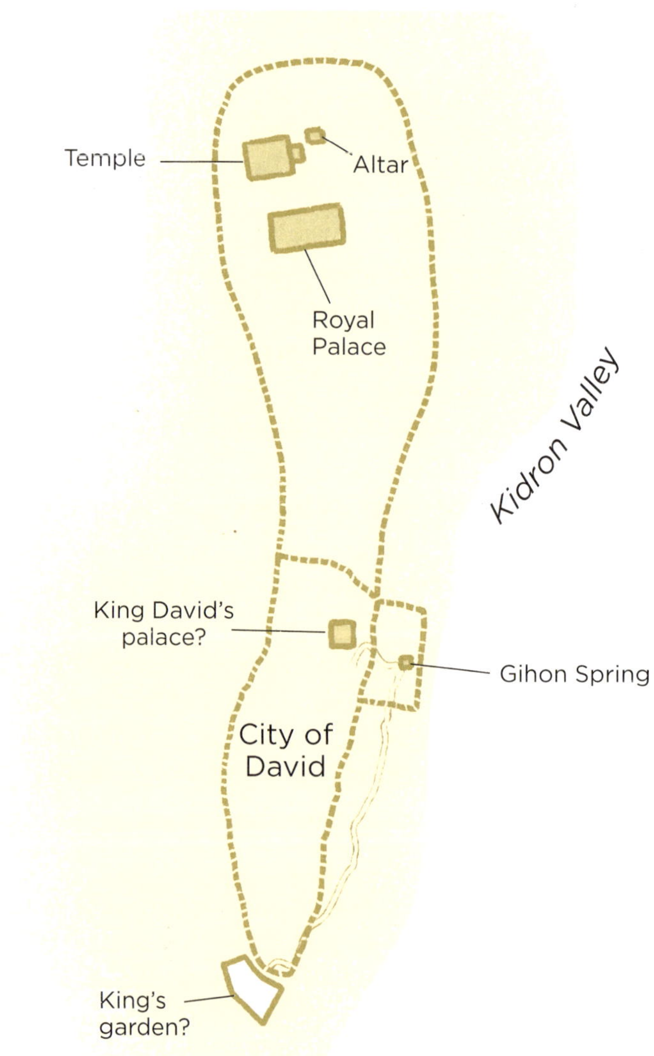

THEMES

Worship is the overarching theme of these psalms, worship offered in praise and thanksgiving for God's faithfulness to his people. Another major theme is trust. Learning to trust God through the varied pains and perplexities of life is part of every believer's life journey. Finally, what permeates this entire collection of psalms is joy. We learn from those traveling pilgrims that joy is possible in every difficulty and challenge we face when our destination is the presence of God.

STUDYING THE PSALMS OF ASCENTS

The fifteen Psalms of Ascents are a collection, but each psalm is its own entity. Before you begin each week's lesson, read the entire psalm all the way through (most of them are quite short!)

> *"The soul travels its affections. If you are in love with the earth, your journey is taking you far from God. If you are in love with God, you are climbing toward him."*[2]

GROUP STUDY

If you are doing this study as part of a group, you'll want to finish each week's lesson before the group meeting. You can work your way through the study questions all in one sitting or by doing a little bit each day. And don't be discouraged if you don't have sufficient time to answer every question. Just do as much as you can, knowing that the more you do, the more you'll learn. No matter how much of the study you are able to complete each week, the group will benefit simply from your presence, so don't skip the gathering because you can't finish! That being said, group time will be most rewarding for every participant if you have done the lesson in advance.

If you are leading the group, scan the QR code below or visit crossway.org/AscentsLeadersGuide/ to download a free leader's guide with study tips and answers to discussion questions.

INDIVIDUAL STUDY

The study is designed to run for ten weeks, but you can set your own pace if you're studying solo. And you can download the free leader's guide if you'd like some guidance along the way.

Marinating in the Scripture text is the most important part of any Bible study.

Reading Plan

	Primary Text	Supplemental Reading
Week 1	Psalm 120	Genesis 12:1–4; Habakkuk 2:4
Week 2	Psalm 121	
Week 3	Psalm 122	Genesis 15:1–6; Psalm 32
Week 4	Psalms 123–124	Genesis 3:1–19
Week 5	Psalms 125–126	
Week 6	Psalms 127–128	Galatians 5:16–26
Week 7	Psalm 129	
Week 8	Psalms 130–131	
Week 9	Psalm 132	
Week 10	Psalms 133–134	Genesis 3:14–15

WEEK 1

LONGING FOR HOME

PSALM 120

Homesickness is a longing for home, for all that's familiar. But it's more than just longing. To be *sick* for *home* is to feel cut off from the easy comforts and let-your-guard-down acceptance of the people we love most. Home is a place, but even more, it's the people—family and friends—who anchor our identity. For disciples of Christ, God intends that the fullest expression of everything we associate with home is to be found in the church, in the fellowship of his people. If you've known this rich blessing, then you know the ache of extended time away from your faith community. Even short separations can trigger the ache, those days when your only company is unbelievers whose plans and purposes revolve around selfish pursuits and worldly pleasures. Psalm 120 was penned by someone in just such a circumstance—stranded in a godless place. As the first in the Psalms of Ascents collection, perhaps it was sung when God's people were in the beginning stages of their journey to Jerusalem.

THE BIG PICTURE (PSALM 120)

A Song of Ascents.

1 In my distress I called to the Lord,
    and he answered me.
2 Deliver me, O Lord,
    from lying lips,
    from a deceitful tongue.

3 What shall be given to you,
and what more shall be done to you,
you deceitful tongue?
4 A warrior's sharp arrows,
with glowing coals of the broom tree!

5 Woe to me, that I sojourn in Meshech,
that I dwell among the tents of Kedar!
6 Too long have I had my dwelling
among those who hate peace.
7 I am for peace,
but when I speak, they are for war! (Psalm 120)

1. What key words are used more than once in the psalm? Note any initial impressions these repeated words provide you.

LONGING FOR DELIVERANCE (vv. 1–2)

The weary psalmist remembers God's faithfulness in times past, which gives him confidence to cry out for deliverance in the present:

1 In my distress I called to the Lord,
and he answered me.
2 Deliver me, O Lord,
from lying lips,
from a deceitful tongue. (vv. 1–2)

The psalmist uses God's covenant name, Yahweh, which is indicated in the Bible whenever "Lord" appears like this, in small capital letters. This isn't a minor detail! Wrapped up in the name Yahweh is everything God promised (covenanted) to be and do for Israel, his people—provide for all their needs and protect them from every enemy. They, in turn, were to give him their love and loyalty by obeying his ways, which were set out for them in the law of Moses. God's people failed to keep the covenant, but God remained faithful. By drawing on God's covenant name in his present predicament, the psalmist is reminded of God's faithfulness, and it gives him confidence that God will not forsake him now or ever.

The psalmist asks to be delivered from "lying lips" and a "deceitful tongue." We aren't told the specific situation, but it's clear that someone was stirring up trouble with untruthful words.

2. Think about an occasion when someone lied to you. How did it impact you and perhaps your relationship with the one who lied?

3. Many of us tend at times to downplay the destructive nature of dishonesty. We water down its awful impact when we call it "exaggeration" or "embellishment" or "white lie," but Scripture paints a vivid picture of its effects. Fill in the following Lies and Liars chart and then write a summary statement of how the Bible portrays dishonesty.

Lies and Liars	
	What Do You Learn?
Psalms 5:6; 7:14	
Proverbs 6:16–19	

Lies and Liars	
	What Do You Learn?
Proverbs 19:5	
Proverbs 26:28	
John 8:44	
Colossians 3:9	
Revelation 21:8	

- Summary statement:

4. What is indicated in verses 1–2 about the psalmist's state of mind as he begins his prayer?

LONGING FOR JUSTICE (vv. 3–4)

Now the psalmist expresses his reflection directly to the liar:

> 3 What shall be given to you,
> and what more shall be done to you,
> you deceitful tongue?
> 4 A warrior's sharp arrows,
> with glowing coals of the broom tree! (vv. 3–4)

5. The psalmist is most likely expressing righteous anger in these verses. At the same time, the verses could serve as a warning to the liar, revealing what he can expect for unrepentant sin. What do the images in these verses convey about what awaits unrepentant sinners?

6. Read Psalm 11:5–7, another passage where burning coals are used as a word picture. What does the image of burning coals in these psalms show us about God?

7. It's right to be angry at sin, although it's very hard to be sinlessly angry. Until we are perfected in glory, the time when we will finally be free from all the effects of sin, it's doubtful that we can experience purely righteous anger. How can adopting the psalmist's perspective help us?

Broom Tree

The broom tree is a bush with many branches and twigs, small leaves, and clusters of flowers.[3]

8. Jesus said that Satan is a liar and the father of lies. How does Revelation 12:9 reveal the fate of this father of lies—the way in which this psalm will ultimately be fulfilled?

LONGING FOR PEACE (vv. 5–7)

As the psalm draws to a close, we get a bit more insight into the source of the psalmist's distress:

> 5 Woe to me, that I sojourn in Meshech,
> that I dwell among the tents of Kedar!
> 6 Too long have I had my dwelling
> among those who hate peace.
> 7 I am for peace,
> but when I speak, they are for war! (vv. 5–7)

Meshech and Kedar refer to two people groups. Meshech was north of Israel and Kedar to the southeast. Since the psalmist obviously couldn't dwell in both places at once, it's best to take verse 5 as a general reference to his living among unbelieving Gentiles.

9. How is the psalmist's living situation affecting him?

Given the psalmist's lament in verses 5–7, some Bible scholars think that Psalm 120 was written during what's called "the exile," the time when God's people were forcibly taken from their homeland and carried away captive to Babylon. During the exile, God's people were compelled to live among idol-worshiping pagans and to conform to the Babylonian way of life. Although God brought this judgment on his people for their unfaithfulness, he intended to use the exile for good, both for his people and for the pagans who captured them. Other Bible scholars think that Psalm 120 was written after the exile, when God's people were allowed to return to their homeland. After they returned, there was still a lot of intermingling between God's people and other nations, and the challenges of that time are certainly reflected in this psalm. Whatever the origins of the psalm, it comforted wandering Israel when they were far from Jerusalem, the symbolic center of God's presence in those days.

10. Pictured in Psalm 120 are two completely polarized worldviews. The psalmist seeks to promote peace, but the unbelieving Gentiles (non-Israelites) have a thirst for conflict. What do you think is the only lasting remedy for this conflict?

11. How would you summarize what the psalmist is longing for?

12. Until Jesus returns, there will always be spiritual conflict between God's people and those who reject him. How do the following passages help us apply Psalm 120 to our lives today?

- 2 Corinthians 6:14–18

- 1 Peter 2:11–12

Festival Fact

"The Israelites kept three pilgrim feasts—Unleavened Bread, Harvest, and Ingathering. Each annual festival testified to the grace of God. Unleavened Bread reminded God's people of the night they left Egypt, and thus it spoke of their salvation. Harvest and Ingathering both celebrated the bounty of God's provision: The God who saves is a God who provides . . . The worship year began with unleavened bread and ended with lavish feasting."[4]

13. The psalmist found solace in journeying to Jerusalem to worship with God's people. How do we apply this in our own day?

LET'S TALK

1. Describe a time when you were homesick. What were the circumstances that led to it, and why did you want to go home? Discuss what earthly homesickness reveals about our spiritual, eternal homesickness and what present provision God has made for us.

2. We live in the midst of unbelievers at work, in school, and in our neighborhoods. As we intermingle, we can blend in by adopting their worldly ways, or we can stand out from them by upholding God's ways. Discuss the ramifications of both.

3. Revelation 12:9 calls Satan "the deceiver of the whole world." He lies and loves to promote lying, especially lies about God. We see the havoc he causes in the way lies destroy relationships and harm trust in God. Think about a time when you lied to someone or when someone lied to you. How was this spiritual truth about lies and liars exposed in the process?

WEEK 2

KEPT FOREVER

PSALM 121

Travelers in our day go place to place in air-conditioned comfort, lounging in ergonomically engineered seats with every conceivable amenity at the touch of a button. That was hardly the situation of God's people making the trek to Jerusalem. Their journey was no doubt a wearying experience, often a perilous one. Undertaking the long, slow trip meant exposure to the elements night and day, attacks by unscrupulous characters, unexpected medical crises, and the relentless feeding of families and animals. Even so, they persevered. What kept them moving forward on the journey to Jerusalem? That's what Psalm 121 is all about—not merely persevering but having *confidence* to persevere. What gives you confidence for your journey, not merely a road trip but the journey of life itself? Let's think about that as we work through this week's lesson.

THE BIG PICTURE (PSALM 121)

A Song of Ascents.

1 I lift up my eyes to the hills.
From where does my help come?
2 My help comes from the LORD,
who made heaven and earth.

3 He will not let your foot be moved;
he who keeps you will not slumber.

4 Behold, he who keeps Israel
will neither slumber nor sleep.

5 The LORD is your keeper;
the LORD is your shade on your right hand.
6 The sun shall not strike you by day,
nor the moon by night.

7 The LORD will keep you from all evil;
he will keep your life.
8 The LORD will keep
your going out and your coming in
from this time forth and forevermore. (Psalm 121)

The psalmist used great skill in how he structured these eight short verses. He made use of some really cool poetry features that help us understand what he's telling us about God. One of these is a technique called "step parallelism," where a word is repeated to give the effect of stepping up.[5]

1. Notice how the psalmist uses "step parallelism" right out of the gate, where the word "help" appears in both verses 1 and 2. In what way is help *stepped up* from verse 1 to verse 2?

2. What key words appear more than once in the psalm? Note any initial impressions you get from these repeated words.

3. List all that the psalmist says about who God is and/or what God does:

	The Lord is . . .	The Lord will . . .
v. 3		
v. 4		
v. 5		
v. 6		
v. 7		
v. 8		

ALWAYS HELPING (vv. 1–2)

The psalmist's reflection begins with a look:

> 1 I lift up my eyes to the hills.
> From where does my help come?
> 2 My help comes from the LORD,
> who made heaven and earth. (vv. 1–2)

As he journeys, he looks up at the surrounding landscape. We aren't told what hills he sees. Perhaps he is drawing close to Jerusalem, and the hills that surround the city come into view. On the other hand, "the hills" might represent an unnamed danger. In the Old Testament, idols were worshiped at sites known as the "high places." Again and again, God's own people turned away from him in order to participate in the evil that occurred at these high places. They wrongly believed that a bit of idol worship was a good idea—if God wouldn't meet all their needs, well, serving an idol seemed the best way to hedge their bets.

4. The same word translated as "lift up" in verse 1 is translated as "cast her eyes on" in Genesis 39:6–7, where we're told that "Joseph was handsome in form and appearance. And after a time his master's wife *cast her eyes* on Joseph and said, 'Lie with me.'" Despite these different translations, the basic meaning of the word is the same. How does the way that the term is used in Genesis shed light on the psalmist's state of mind when he uses the term in verse 1?

"Surely our anxieties come only as we lose sight of the greatness and goodness of God."[6]

We already considered the way that the word *help* is "stepped up" from verse 1 to verse 2. The psalmist asks, "From where does my help come?" in verse 1 not because he's perplexed and desperate but because he's setting us up for the answer in verse 2.[7]

5. In verse 2 the psalmist identifies the Lord as the one "who made heaven and earth." How does identifying the Lord as Creator of everything show us the answer to his question in verse 1?

ALWAYS WATCHING (vv. 3–4)

The psalmist gives more reasons why God's people have no need to fear:

> 3 He will not let your foot be moved;
>   he who keeps you will not slumber.
> 4 Behold, he who keeps Israel
>   will neither slumber nor sleep. (vv. 3–4)

6. What do you think the psalmist means when he writes that God "will not let your foot be moved"? Take a look at Psalm 40:1–3 and Proverbs 3:25–26 if you want some help with your answer.

In verse 4 we find a *pleonasm*, a poetic technique in which a word or idea is used twice as a way to convey size or scale or scope. So when the psalmist writes that God "neither slumbers nor sleeps," he's saying that God's care for his people is constant.[8]

7. Sleep—or sleeplessness—plagues many of us from time to time (or, in some cases, on a regular basis). Insomnia occurs for a variety of reasons. Sometimes the underlying cause is physiological, like when our hormones are out of whack. Other times, the cause of sleeplessness is stress or anxiety, which can indicate a spiritual component. What are we told in verse 4 that can break the tyranny of anxiety-induced insomnia?

8. Remember that the psalmist is now elaborating on the question and answer with which he opened the psalm: "From where does my help come? My help comes from the LORD." Summarize what you learn from verses 3–4 about how the Lord helps his people.

ALWAYS KEEPING (vv. 5–6)

The psalmist tells us more about who God is:

> 5 The LORD is your keeper;
> the LORD is your shade on your right hand.
> 6 The sun shall not strike you by day,
> nor the moon by night. (vv. 5–6)

Another poetic technique known as *merism* is found here. A merism is when polar opposites are used together to indicate completeness. "By day . . . by night" is a merism indicating "all the time."[9]

9. Based on the psalm as a whole, what do think it means that God is our "keeper"?

10. Think about what shade provides. With this word, what is the psalmist saying in a poetic way about one of the ways the Lord "keeps" us?

11. Verses 5–6 actually point forward in time to the way God has planned for the ultimate "keeping" of his people in the new heavens and the new earth. We see this in Revelation 7:15–17. What more do we discover in that passage about what God has prepared for the people he keeps?

Festival Fact

The Feast of Unleavened Bread looked back to the exodus, when God brought his people out of bondage. "For centuries they had served as slaves in Egypt, but God delivered them . . . On the night that Pharaoh finally let God's people go, the Israelites had to leave in such a hurry that they didn't even have time to let their bread rise . . . To remind them of this, God gave the people a feast of remembrance. Every year when they ate their unleavened bread, the festival would call to mind their exodus from Egypt."[10]

KEPT FOREVER (vv. 7–8)

We reach the last "step" of the psalm in these final verses. The phrase "your going out and your coming in" refers to the activities of daily life.

> 7 The Lord will keep you from all evil;
> he will keep your life.
> 8 The Lord will keep
> your going out and your coming in
> from this time forth and forevermore. (vv. 7–8)

12. The Lord protects his people from evil, and the ways in which we are protected are revealed all through his word. The means God uses to protect us often include our own participation. Fill in the Kept from Evil chart to learn more about how God keeps us from evil.

Kept from Evil	
	Means of Protection
Matthew 6:9–13	
John 10:27–28	
Romans 8:31–39	
Ephesians 6:10–18	
James 4:7–8	
1 Peter 5:6–9	
Jude 24–25	

13. Verse 8 gets us to the very top of the psalmist's "steps." How does the last line of the psalm demonstrate this?

LET'S TALK

1. Travelers to Jerusalem sang this psalm to strengthen their confidence to complete the journey. In the big-picture scheme of things, we too are on a journey, traveling from this life to our eternal home in heaven. Describe how a right view of God and his involvement in the lives of his people encourages you to persevere today in some particular way.

2. How do Jesus's words in Matthew 6:25–34 help you know how to apply all the psalmist says in Psalm 121?

3. In a sermon preached by the apostle Peter, we're told concerning Jesus that "there is salvation in no one else, for there is no other name under heaven given among men by which we must be saved" (Acts 4:12). This means that all the details we're given in Psalm 121 about the Lord's care for his people are true for everyone united to Christ by faith. As you consider the psalm, talk about some of the specific blessings that accompany our salvation.

WEEK 3

GATHERED TOGETHER

PSALM 122

If you've ever watched the movie *The Wizard of Oz*, it's likely you recall the poignant scene when the homesick Dorothy clicks the heels of her ruby slippers together and chants, "There's no place like home ... there's no place like home."[11] The scene stands out to us because we get it; we've known her longing ourselves. In the psalm we're studying this week, Dorothy's chant has become a reality for God's people. They've arrived at Jerusalem. Their arduous journey is over. The city was the most precious place on earth for Israel. The glory of God's presence was set there, first in the tent, or tabernacle, that served as the center of their worship, and later in the great temple. Upon reaching the city, the journeying Israelites arrived at the home of their hearts. For those of us in Christ, the same delight is meant for us as we gather together for worship. If we're honest, though, we have to admit that the effort to gather with our Christian family is sometimes more delightful in theory than in practice. Getting the kids dressed and out the door on Sunday mornings can frazzle our hearts, and even when morning preparation goes smoothly, some weeks we just don't feel like going. Studying Psalm 122 renews our zeal for corporate worship, but even more, it points us to the time when it will be the most joyous experience we can imagine.

THE BIG PICTURE (PSALM 122)

A Song of Ascents. Of David.

1 I was glad when they said to me,
"Let us go to the house of the Lord!"

2 Our feet have been standing
    within your gates, O Jerusalem!

3 Jerusalem—built as a city
    that is bound firmly together,
4 to which the tribes go up,
    the tribes of the Lord,
as was decreed for Israel,
    to give thanks to the name of the Lord.
5 There thrones for judgment were set,
    the thrones of the house of David.

6 Pray for the peace of Jerusalem!
    "May they be secure who love you!
7 Peace be within your walls
    and security within your towers!"
8 For my brothers and companions' sake
    I will say, "Peace be within you!"
9 For the sake of the house of the Lord our God,
    I will seek your good. (Psalm 122)

The superscription or title of this psalm is "A Song of Ascents. Of David," which indicates that Israel's great King David wrote it. If he was indeed the author, the psalm might tie directly to an event in David's life that's recorded for us in 1 Chronicles 15–16. If that's the case, the psalm was likely written to commemorate this occasion in Chronicles, and then sung by later generations of God's people who came to Jerusalem. Others think the superscription "of David" in the title means that it was written not *by* David but *in the tradition of* David years later. In either case, what matters for us is not the author of the psalm but the Lord it takes us to.

1. Note the repeated words or phrases in Psalm 122 that stand out to you.

2. The phrase “the house of the LORD” occurs in both the first and last verses of the psalm. What do you think the psalmist is communicating through the placement of this repeated phrase?

3. As you consider the psalm as a whole, what initial impressions do you get of Jerusalem as it was in the psalmist’s day?

GLADNESS IN THE GATES (vv. 1–2)

The psalmist begins by taking us from his recent past into his present:

> 1 I was glad when they said to me,
> “Let us go to the house of the LORD!”
> 2 Our feet have been standing
> within your gates, O Jerusalem! (vv. 1–2)

4. In verse 1, he looks back on the beginning of his journey to Jerusalem. What encouraged him to embark on the trip?

5. Why do you think the prospect of going to the house of the Lord in Jerusalem brought gladness to the psalmist's heart?

> **City Gates**
>
> The gates of a walled city were the entry point to safety. Citizens and travelers congregated at the gates to socialize and gather news. Judicial proceedings were conducted at the gates as well, attended by the elders and leading citizens of the city.

6. Where does the psalmist locate himself in the present?

CITY ON A HILL (vv. 3–5)

We find in these verses more of the "step parallelism" that we first encountered in Psalm 121. If you recall, step parallelism is when a word is repeated to give the effect of intensifying or *stepping up* its meaning:

3 Jerusalem—built as a city
  that is bound firmly together,
4 to which the tribes go up,
  the tribes of the LORD,
as was decreed for Israel,
  to give thanks to the name of the LORD.

5 There thrones for judgment were set,
the thrones of the house of David. (vv. 3–5)

7. How are each of the following words "stepped up" in verses 3–5?

   - Tribes:

   - Thrones:

The tribes are a reference to what were originally the twelve tribes of Israel, who descended from the twelve sons of the patriarch Jacob. Over the centuries the tribes rose and fell, united and divided, and through it all, the tribe of Judah rose to the premier place, the tribe from which came both King David and Jesus himself.

8. What is indicated about Jerusalem in each of these three verses?

   - v. 3

   - v. 4

- v. 5

Jerusalem

"Jerusalem became a Jewish city and achieved biblical prominence under King David, who wrested it from the Jebusites and made it both his political and religious capital. He made it a political center by constructing his palace and other governmental buildings there (see 2 Sam. 5:6–12). He made it the Jews' religious center by bringing the ark of the covenant to Jerusalem, a story told at length in 2 Samuel 6 and 1 Chronicles 15 and 16. It was placed within the relocated tabernacle. Later Solomon built the glorious golden temple, which David had wanted to build, and the ark was placed in its Most Holy Place. The temple thus became the center of the city, which was the center of the nation."[12]

It was King David who established Jerusalem as the center of life for God's people. "Jerusalem was a border town that belonged to none of the existing tribes. So by choosing it as his capital, David chose a city that would belong to the entire nation. Here people from each of the tribes could go up and know that he or she belonged to one united people."[13] We see echoes of this all through Psalm 122.

9. What does verse 4 reveal as the primary purpose for undertaking the journey to Jerusalem?

Jerusalem "Bound Firmly Together"[14]

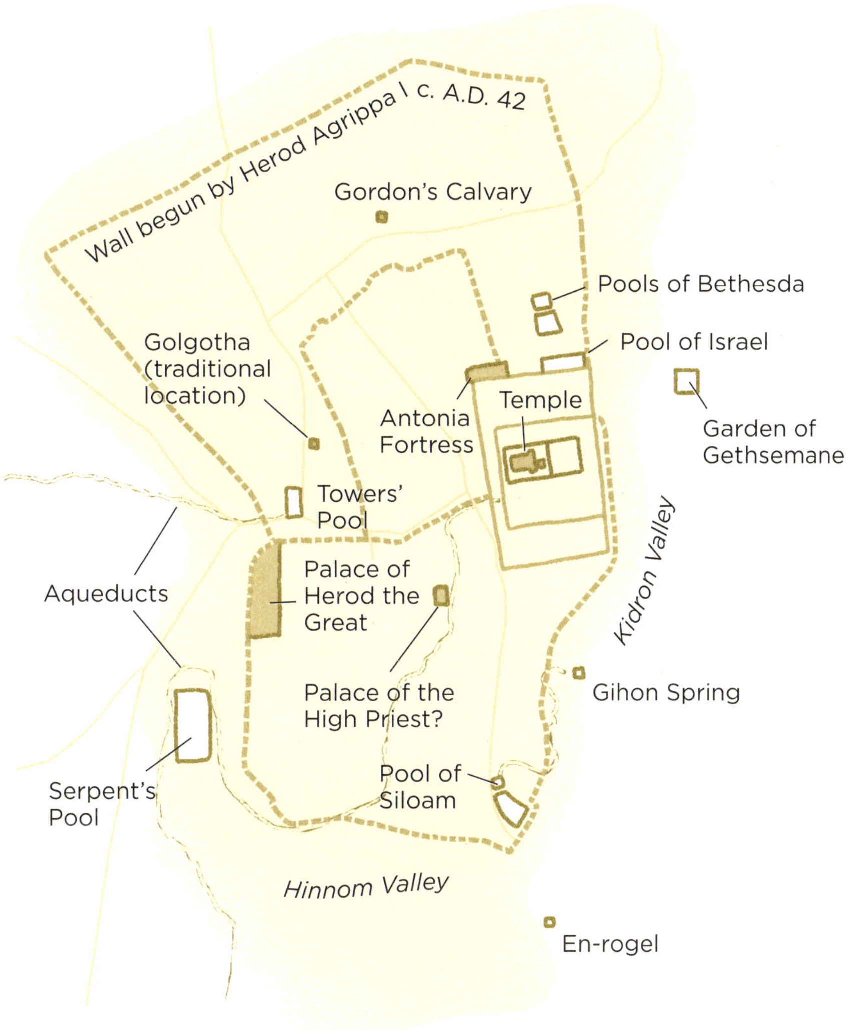

The "thrones for judgment" in verse 5 show us that Jerusalem was not only the center for worship but also for legal justice. The city was the government seat of Israel. It might seem odd to include this detail in a psalm primarily about worshiping the Lord, but all through the Bible we're shown that "dispensing justice is one of the two God-given functions of right government. The other is defending its citizens against violence. When the kings of Israel took this responsibility seriously and gave just judgments, the city and nation were blessed by God and prospered."[15]

10. How do the psalmist's words about Jerusalem in verses 3–5 enhance your understanding of why the psalmist is glad to finally be there?

11. Being in Jerusalem fills the psalmist with gladness. It's clear that it satisfies his heart. How does John 1:14 reveal the way believers today share in that same satisfaction?

PRAY FOR PEACE! (VV. 6–9)

As we come to these final verses, the psalmist pours out his hope for God's blessing on Jerusalem:

> 6 Pray for the peace of Jerusalem!
> "May they be secure who love you!
> 7 Peace be within your walls
> and security within your towers!"
> 8 For my brothers and companions' sake
> I will say, "Peace be within you!"
> 9 For the sake of the house of the LORD our God,
> I will seek your good. (vv. 6–9)

12. As king, David was responsible for the welfare of the city and its occupants. What motivates his pursuit of peace in these verses?

13. How does the psalmist view himself in relation to all those who set their sight on Jerusalem?

The "house" mentioned in verse 9 is the tabernacle, which contained the ark of the covenant. If you recall, this "house" is where God chose to set his presence and to meet with his people. Once King David established Jerusalem as his capital city, he desired to replace the portable tabernacle with a big, beautiful temple for the Lord. David's hope for such a temple did come true, but not until the reign of his son Solomon.

Festival Fact

The second feast requiring pilgrimage occurred in early summer. "This feast—also known as the Feast of Firstfruits—was carefully timed. When the grain was ready for harvest, the Israelites would take the first sheaf of wheat and wave it before the Lord (Lev. 23:9–11) as a way of acknowledging that the whole harvest came from him. This was done on the day after a Sabbath, but it was only the beginning. Next the Israelites would count off seven full weeks, which explains why the celebration had yet another name: the Feast of Weeks. Then on the fiftieth day the people would bring an offering to their God. The main thing the Israelites offered was bread . . . representing the fullness of the harvest."[16]

LET'S TALK

1. The delight of the psalmist on reaching Jerusalem foreshadows the joy we are meant to have as we gather to worship in church with our brothers and sisters in Christ. Where do you see echoes of the themes of Psalm 122 in your church? How can you follow the psalmist's lead in seeking its good?

2. We pray for individuals in our church, but we learn from the psalm that it's important to pray for the church as a whole. This includes the well-being of our own churches and for the church worldwide (all true believers everywhere in the world belong to the one universal church). Talk about how Psalm 122 can shape our prayers for the church, beginning with our own and spreading out across the nation and the world.

3. Psalm 122 emphasizes the blessing of peace. Talk about the way God's peace differs from the world's idea of peace. You might want to look at John 14:27; Romans 8:6; 14:17–19; Ephesians 2:13–19; and Hebrews 12:14.

WEEK 4

MIGHTY TO SAVE

PSALMS 123–124

Every journey has ups and downs, highs and lows—a reality that comes into sharp focus this week as we consider Psalms 123 and 124 in a single lesson. (Given that there are fifteen Psalms of Ascents in a ten-week Bible study, some doubling up is necessary.) Psalm 123 shows us a low point, a time when God's people were battling discouragement. Even so, right in the midst of it, they turn to the Lord for help. The psalm teaches us to do likewise. In the midst of our own difficulties, we'll find the help we need when we take our eyes off our problems and fix our gaze on God. Then, in Psalm 124, we find out why looking at the Lord is always wiser than fixating on our problems. The psalm is a high point, filled with praise for God's faithfulness. Here we see that the Lord sticks with us in every trouble and delivers us.

THE BIG PICTURE (PSALM 123)

A Song of Ascents.

1 To you I lift up my eyes,
O you who are enthroned in the heavens!
2 Behold, as the eyes of servants
look to the hand of their master,
as the eyes of a maidservant
to the hand of her mistress,
so our eyes look to the LORD our God,
till he has mercy upon us.

3 Have mercy upon us, O LORD, have mercy upon us,
for we have had more than enough of contempt.
4 Our soul has had more than enough
of the scorn of those who are at ease,
of the contempt of the proud. (Psalm 123)

1. Jot down the repeated words or phrases in Psalm 123 that stand out to you.

2. As you consider the psalm as a whole, what mood or outlook is expressed here?

EYES LIFTED UP (123:1)

As Israel journeys toward Jerusalem, they direct their hearts to the Lord:

> To you I lift up my eyes,
> O you who are enthroned in the heavens! (123:1)

3. The psalmist lifts his eyes—he directs his desire—to the Lord, who is "enthroned in the heavens." What does this description of the Lord convey about why the psalmist turns to the Lord in his difficulty?

4. What does Revelation 22:1–4 add to your understanding of the Lord's kingly rule?

WANTING AND WAITING (123:2)

The psalmist elaborates on *why* he looks to the Lord, but also on *how* he looks:

> Behold, as the eyes of servants
>   look to the hand of their master,
> as the eyes of a maidservant
>   to the hand of her mistress,
> so our eyes look to the LORD our God,
>   till he has mercy upon us. (123:2)

5. What outlook or posture is conveyed in the psalmist's words?

6. Some Bible commentators have interpreted this verse to mean that the psalmist is waiting for instructions from the Lord, but when we consider the psalm as a whole, and this verse in particular, we come up with a different interpretation of what the psalmist is waiting for. What is it?

7. The psalm gives us a biblical picture of how to wait on the Lord—for answers to prayer, for deliverance from injustice, for relief from trouble. What do we learn from verse 2 about *how* to wait on the Lord?

> *"The goal of the pilgrim is not Jerusalem . . . but God himself, whose true throne is not anywhere on earth but in heaven."*[17]

The psalmist is suffering under the weight of his difficulty. Because that's true, we might wonder why mercy is what he desires from God. We'd expect to see, "Our eyes look to the Lord for relief," or, "Our eyes look to the Lord for deliverance." But both relief and deliverance are bound up in this word *mercy*. The original Hebrew word that is translated here as "mercy" is all about God's lovingkindness toward his people.

MORE THAN ENOUGH! (123:3–4)

Now the psalmist's desire for mercy becomes a specific prayer request:

> 3 Have mercy upon us, O Lord, have mercy upon us,
> for we have had more than enough of contempt.
> 4 Our soul has had more than enough
> of the scorn of those who are at ease,
> of the contempt of the proud. (123:3–4)

8. Based on what you see in verses 3–4, what demonstration of God's mercy do you think the psalmist is requesting?

Contempt

Contempt is "the act of despising." It's a "lack of respect or reverence."[18]

9. What do we learn from the following verses about pride and arrogance?

   - Proverbs 16:5

   - 1 Corinthians 13:4

10. In Psalm 123:4, we see a link between arrogance and contempt. Why do you think that proud people are contemptuous of others?

11. The psalmist's prayer in verses 3–4 points forward to, or foreshadows, what Jesus experienced. In the New Testament we're told that proud people "treated him with contempt and mocked him" (Luke 23:11). Because he was subjected to scorn and contempt, he knows how it feels and has compassion on us when people scorn us.

There's a huge difference, however, between his experience of contempt and ours. As sinners, we deserve contempt. Jesus had no sin. How does Isaiah 53:1–6 explain why Jesus the sinless one was scorned?

THE BIG PICTURE (PSALM 124)

A Song of Ascents. Of David.

1 If it had not been the LORD who was on our side—
let Israel now say—
2 if it had not been the LORD who was on our side
when people rose up against us,
3 then they would have swallowed us up alive,
when their anger was kindled against us;
4 then the flood would have swept us away,
the torrent would have gone over us;
5 then over us would have gone
the raging waters.

6 Blessed be the LORD,
who has not given us
as prey to their teeth!
7 We have escaped like a bird
from the snare of the fowlers;
the snare is broken,
and we have escaped!

8 Our help is in the name of the LORD,
who made heaven and earth. (Psalm 124)

12. We find many vivid nature images in the psalm. What do these images convey?

    - v. 3

    - v. 4

    - v. 5

    - v. 6

    - v. 7

13. Note which part of the psalm is past tense and which is present. How does this show us what's changed in the psalmist's circumstances?

> *"We rejoice that our help is in God, since we are so helpless."*[19]

IF . . . (124:1–5)

These first five verses of Psalm 124 set out a vivid set of "if . . . then" statements:

1 If it had not been the LORD who was on our side—
  let Israel now say—
2 if it had not been the LORD who was on our side
  when people rose up against us,
3 then they would have swallowed us up alive,
  when their anger was kindled against us;
4 then the flood would have swept us away,
  the torrent would have gone over us;
5 then over us would have gone
  the raging waters. (124:1–5)

14. The threat that faced Israel was nothing short of utter calamity. What prevented the calamity from happening?

The Lord Sides with His People

How did Israel know that the Lord was on their side? It seems presumptuous to our ears, doesn't it? But we know it's true because it was God's promise to his people, a promise to redeem them from the destructive forces aligned against them. God's plan to redeem his people is revealed gradually all through the Bible. The first glimpse we're given is all the way back in the garden of Eden, in Genesis, after Adam and Eve sinned. There we're given the first hint of a Redeemer, the "offspring" who would rescue human beings from the consequences of their sin. The hint is seen in God's word to the serpent in Genesis 3:15: "I will put enmity between you and the woman, / and between your offspring and her offspring; / he shall bruise your head, / and you shall bruise his heel."

God's gracious plan of rescue is later revealed in the covenant he made with the patriarch Abraham (see Genesis 12:1–3). Then later, God made a covenant with Moses, the covenant of works, which is summarized in the Ten Commandments. Here, God's people were to obey God's law, and he in turn would protect them under his care. Of course, because they were sinners, they failed to obey, which exposed their very great need for a Savior, someone who could keep the law and please God.

Generations later, God made a covenant with King David (see 2 Samuel 7:8–10). In this case, God established David as the first in a line of kings through whom the long-promised Savior would eventually come. David, in his role as Israel's king, serving under God's authority, was responsible to protect Israel and provide for their needs. He loved the Lord, but he too failed to be faithful. Even so, as the Lord's appointed king, David foreshadowed the eternal King yet to come, the one who'd do what no earthly king ever could—redeem sinners from death and secure them for everlasting joy in God's presence. All the Old Testament covenants and kings in David's line prefigured this one true King, the Lord Jesus Christ. With that big-picture view of God's plan, worked out in the world through his people Israel, we can understand why the psalmist could say with such confidence that the Lord was on Israel's side.

BLESSED ESCAPE (124:6–7)

In verses 1–5, the psalmist was reflecting on God's deliverance of Israel at some earlier time in the past. Now he praises God for this deliverance:

> 6 Blessed be the Lord,
> who has not given us
> as prey to their teeth!
> 7 We have escaped like a bird
> from the snare of the fowlers;

the snare is broken,
    and we have escaped! (124:6–7)

15. Israel rejoices in their deliverance from a danger unknown to us, but their rescue foreshadows a much greater deliverance that we do know, one that reaches way beyond Israel. Note how each passage in the Deliverance chart reveals this greater rescue.

Deliverance

	Who Delivers Us	What We're Delivered From
Romans 5:6–9		
Romans 7:22–25a		
1 Corinthians 15:25–26		
Hebrews 2:14–15		

The Lord Jesus's life was threatened, but he wasn't rescued. He was handed over to his enemies as "prey to their teeth." Israel was unfaithful to God, so, unlike Jesus, they deserved destruction. So do we. But Jesus took on himself the destruction we deserve. If we have placed our faith in Jesus, we can say with Israel, "The snare is broken, and we have escaped!"

WHAT'S IN A NAME? (124:8)

The psalm ends with a joyful declaration:

Our help is in the name of the Lord,
    who made heaven and earth. (124:8)

Notice where the psalmist sets his hope—not just in the Lord but in the "name" of the Lord. There are many names for God in the Bible, but the one used here in verse 8—Yahweh, or "I AM"—was the most important to Israel because it was God's *covenant* name. It's the name in view whenever we see LORD with small capital letters. It was given back in the days of Moses, when Moses said to God, "If I come to the people of Israel and . . . they ask me, 'What is his name?' what shall I say to them?" And the Lord responded, "Say this to the people of Israel: 'I AM has sent me to you. . . . This is my name forever, and thus I am to be remembered throughout all generations'" (Exodus 3:13–15).

Festival Fact

"The Feast of Harvest was a time of joyful celebration. The Israelites offered rich sacrifices unto God. They rested from all their work. And they gathered for public worship, praising God as their provider and thanking him for their daily bread."[20]

16. On another occasion the Lord appeared to Moses and after some necessary preparation, he revealed his glory. Read what happened then in Exodus 34:6–7. How does that incident from Exodus help us understand why Israel hopes in this name?

17. The psalmist's declaration, "Our help is in the name of the LORD, who made heaven and earth," is another part of the psalm that points far into the future. How does John 8:58 show us where the psalmist's declaration ultimately points?

LET'S TALK

1. In Psalm 123, God's people, longing for deliverance from deeply troubling circumstances, look to him for relief—for all that comes to us through his mercy. How can this psalm guide the way you respond to troubles in your own life? Include in your discussion Hebrews 12:2–3, an ideal passage for applying this psalm personally.

2. Israel knew the name of the Lord as Yahweh, "I AM." This is why the psalmist declares, "Our help is in the name of the LORD" (124:8). We have a much fuller understanding of this great name from all Jesus revealed about himself as "I AM" (John 6:35; 8:12; 10:9–11; 11:25–26; 14:6; and 15:5). Look up one or more of those verses in John and talk about how Jesus's revelation of himself as "I AM" shapes the way you think about this psalm and how you might use it for personal prayer.

3. We want to keep in mind as we study that God's people sang the Psalms of Ascents as they journeyed to Jerusalem to worship the Lord and participate in celebratory feasting. What practices might you, or maybe you and your family, work into your routine to help you prepare for worship each week?

WEEK 5

GOODNESS GUARANTEED

PSALMS 125–126

The drive from Chicago east to Central New York takes 11 hours and 36 minutes, barring unexpected traffic jams and no more than two quick stops for gas. That was my experience, anyway. Ten hours into the trip, I was so over it—weary, achy, and bored. But as soon as I saw those first foothills of the Adirondack Mountains, my spirits lifted, and with renewed energy, I completed that final stretch. God's people must have experienced something similar as they neared the end of their journey to Jerusalem. The long trek, uphill no less—talk about weary! But the mountains appearing on the horizon surely put a fresh spring in their step. The joy awaiting them in the city would soon be theirs. Perhaps this is when they sang Psalm 125. The mighty mountain peaks all around Jerusalem were a visual reminder of their security in the Lord. In the same way, we know the Lord Jesus as the rock of our security. Psalm 126, which we'll also study this week, reflects on a happy occasion of divine deliverance and then looks ahead with confident hope for more blessing. Both psalms teach us that even when our journey through life is wearying and painful, we have every reason for joy and can be confident of getting safely to our final destination.

THE BIG PICTURE (PSALM 125)

A Song of Ascents.

1 Those who trust in the LORD are like Mount Zion,
which cannot be moved, but abides forever.

2 As the mountains surround Jerusalem,
so the LORD surrounds his people,
from this time forth and forevermore.
3 For the scepter of wickedness shall not rest
on the land allotted to the righteous,
lest the righteous stretch out
their hands to do wrong.
4 Do good, O LORD, to those who are good,
and to those who are upright in their hearts!
5 But those who turn aside to their crooked ways
the LORD will lead away with evildoers!
Peace be upon Israel! (Psalm 125)

1. What comparisons and contrasts do you notice in Psalm 125?

- Comparisons:

- Contrasts:

2. How would you characterize the psalmist's posture toward the Lord in this psalm?

SAFELY SURROUNDED (125:1–2)

Jerusalem was built on a hill that sits lower than the mountains that surround the city. This is the view that God's journeying people would have seen as they approached their destination, causing them to burst into song:

> 1 Those who trust in the LORD are like Mount Zion,
> which cannot be moved, but abides forever.
> 2 As the mountains surround Jerusalem,
> so the LORD surrounds his people,
> from this time forth and forevermore. (125:1–2)

3. Why, according to the psalmist, can the Lord be trusted?

4. What do you learn from the following passages about how the Lord surrounds and protects his people?

    - Psalm 139:5–10

    - Proverbs 16:9

- Romans 8:28–39

- Ephesians 3:20–21

WHEN EVIL RISES UP (125:3)

The reason that the Lord protectively surrounds his people is revealed in verse 3:

> For the scepter of wickedness shall not rest
>   on the land allotted to the righteous,
> lest the righteous stretch out
>   their hands to do wrong. (125:3)

A *scepter* is a staff held in the hand of a ruler that symbolizes his authority. Here the psalmist uses "scepter of wickedness" to refer to evil rulers. Israel lived constantly under the threat of hostile takeovers by foreign powers, but danger also threatened when wicked Israelite kings ruled God's people.

5. It's easy to understand the threat posed by foreign enemies, but just as much vigilance is needed when evil rules closer to home. According to verse 3, what temptation can afflict people who are subject to evil rulers?

6. What promise is given in verse 3?

7. The psalmist expresses confidence that God has always been faithful to deliver his people from evil oppression, wherever it arises, in his perfect way and time. How does the prayer in Ephesians 1:15–22 paint a fuller picture of what is promised in Psalm 125:3 and what underlies the confidence of God's people in every age?

8. While it's always been challenging for Christians to live under secular powers, one of the greatest difficulties we face is not conforming to the worldly environment foisted upon us under those secular powers. How do the following passages encourage us?

    - Romans 12:2

    - 1 Peter 1:13–16

- 1 John 2:15–17

GOD'S GOODNESS (125:4–5)

The psalm ends with a prayer, a pronouncement, and a petition for peace:

> 4 Do good, O Lord, to those who are good,
> and to those who are upright in their hearts!
> 5 But those who turn aside to their crooked ways
> the Lord will lead away with evildoers!
> Peace be upon Israel! (125:4–5)

The psalmist prays for God's goodness to shower down upon people who are "good" and "upright in their hearts," by which he means God's own people who live in covenant relationship with him.

9. What warning is held out to those who reject God to embrace the ways of the world?

"There is no end to the good things God has prepared for those who have been made righteous by the work of Christ, and it is proper for us to pray for an abundance of good things, as the psalmist does."[21]

Who among us hasn't at times succumbed to worldly temptation or compromised faithfulness in fear of rejection or loss? We all have! We all stand in need of deliverance from the evil that assails us, be it from the world, the flesh (our very own sinfulness), or the devil. That's why the last verse of the psalm, verse 5, is just what we need to share in the psalmist's confidence. His last words are "both a prayer ('*May* peace *be* upon Israel') and a confident prophecy ('Peace *will be* upon Israel'),"[22] and these words are for all God's people in every age, because "now in Christ Jesus you who once were far off have been brought near by the blood of Christ. For he himself is our peace" (Ephesians 2:13–14).

THE BIG PICTURE (PSALM 126)

A Song of Ascents.

1 When the LORD restored the fortunes of Zion,
we were like those who dream.
2 Then our mouth was filled with laughter,
and our tongue with shouts of joy;
then they said among the nations,
"The LORD has done great things for them."
3 The LORD has done great things for us;
we are glad.

4 Restore our fortunes, O LORD,
like streams in the Negeb!
5 Those who sow in tears
shall reap with shouts of joy!
6 He who goes out weeping,
bearing the seed for sowing,
shall come home with shouts of joy,
bringing his sheaves with him. (Psalm 126)

10. Identify the repeated words and phrases in Psalm 126.

11. How does the outlook of the psalmist change from the beginning of the psalm to the end?

A LOOK BACK (126:1–3)

The psalmist reflects on a time when the Lord spectacularly delivered his people from trouble and restored lost blessings:

> 1 When the LORD restored the fortunes of Zion,
> we were like those who dream.
> 2 Then our mouth was filled with laughter,
> and our tongue with shouts of joy;
> then they said among the nations,
> "The LORD has done great things for them."
> 3 The LORD has done great things for us;
> we are glad. (126:1–3)

We don't know what occasion the psalmist has in mind here or whether the deliverance Israel experienced was from a natural disaster, such as a plague or a famine, or from an attack of an enemy nation. We don't need to know because what matters here is the *impact* the deliverance had on God's people.

12. How would you summarize Israel's response to the Lord's great deliverance?

13. How did God's blessing of his people serve as a testimony to outsiders?

A LOOK AHEAD (126:4–6)

The emphasis is no longer on past deliverance but on the present and then on what Israel hopes for in the future:

> 4 Restore our fortunes, O LORD,
> like streams in the Negeb!
> 5 Those who sow in tears
> shall reap with shouts of joy!
> 6 He who goes out weeping,
> bearing the seed for sowing,
> shall come home with shouts of joy,
> bringing his sheaves with him. (126:4–6)

14. Turning from reflecting on the past in verses 1–3, what seems to be the present condition of God's people as they pray in verse 4?

15. The "Negeb" was the southernmost part of Judah. The term *negeb* means "dry" or "parched."[23] How does this term help us understand Israel's prayer in verse 4 and what they hope for in verses 5–6?

16. How would you classify the tone Israel takes in verses 5–6?

17. Israel is dependent on God for restoration and blessing, which is clear from their prayer in verse 4. At the same time, God typically answers the prayers of his people through means, often human means. How is this evidenced in verses 5–6?

18. Agricultural images are used to convey spiritual truths in both Old and New Testaments. What do we learn from the farming images in the following passages?

- Hosea 10:12–13

- Matthew 13:1–9, 18–23

- Galatians 6:7–9

- Revelation 14:14–16

Festival Fact

The Feast of Ingathering was linked to harvesttime. "It came in the autumn . . . when all the crops were safely gathered in . . . Like American Thanksgiving, this was the feast of 'harvest home.'" This feast lasted a full week, during which the Israelites lived in makeshift booths made of leaves and branches. This is why the festival was also called the Feast of Booths or the Feast of Tabernacles."[24]

"As Christians we look back on God's great redeeming work in Christ but there is constant need to pray that God would complete what he has begun in us."[25]

LET'S TALK

1. Israel faced oppression from foreign powers and all too often from their very own rulers, but they are no match for the Lord and his good intentions for his people. We have our own threats to contend with—worldly evils, our own sin nature, and the devil himself. Share something you learned from Psalm 125 that helps you depend on God in the evil that threatens or tempts you. Consider how 1 Corinthians 10:12–13 can help you as well.

2. Psalm 126 shows us how remembering God's faithfulness in the past helps us hope for what he will do in times ahead. Do you similarly hope for blessing, or do you tend to doubt God's generosity? Talk about how Psalm 126 is designed to shape our hope.

3. Psalm 126:5 encourages us that "those who sow in tears shall reap with shouts of joy!" We also see sowing and reaping imagery in the New Testament as it applies to the Christian life. In Galatians 6:8–9 we're told, "The one who sows to his own flesh will from the flesh reap corruption, but the one who sows to the Spirit will from the Spirit reap eternal life. And let us not grow weary of doing good, for in due season we will reap, if we do not give up." Discuss some practical ways to sow spiritually and then, based on what you learned from Psalm 126, what you can expect to reap as a result.

WEEK 6

BLESSINGS OF A HAPPY HOME

PSALMS 127–128

There's a reason why those family-based TV programs of an earlier generation have enduring appeal. People of all ages binge-watch shows like *The Waltons* and *Leave It to Beaver* because they portray an ideal—a thriving family stability. Psalms 127 and 128 also show us what an ideal family looks like, but the standards in these families are very different from what's seen on those television shows. These two psalms paint a picture of the domestic flourishing that happens when God is the foundation of a home. In Psalm 127 we're shown that the success of our efforts, at home and anywhere else we invest, is utterly dependent on the Lord. So Psalm 127 shows us what the Lord does, and then, in Psalm 128, we're shown what we are to do in response. Our labor in the Lord matters. Trusting God and seeking to shape our lives and homes by God's word and ways bears rich fruit in our marriages and in the maturing of our children. And godly families, in turn, bless other families and outward from there into the wider family of believers, and ultimately all of society is impacted. These two psalms are classified as "wisdom psalms," and as we study and apply them, we'll find ourselves enjoying the fruit of God's wisdom.

THE BIG PICTURE (PSALM 127)

The heading of Psalm 127 tells us that King Solomon wrote this psalm. (He is also the author of Psalm 72.) According to 2 Samuel 12:25, Solomon was also called Jedidiah, which means "beloved of the Lord." So when he writes in verse 2 that the Lord "gives to his beloved sleep," he might be recalling his own experience.

A Song of Ascents. Of Solomon.

1 Unless the LORD builds the house,
those who build it labor in vain.
Unless the LORD watches over the city,
the watchman stays awake in vain.
2 It is in vain that you rise up early
and go late to rest,
eating the bread of anxious toil;
for he gives to his beloved sleep.

3 Behold, children are a heritage from the LORD,
the fruit of the womb a reward.
4 Like arrows in the hand of a warrior
are the children of one's youth.
5 Blessed is the man
who fills his quiver with them!
He shall not be put to shame
when he speaks with his enemies in the gate. (Psalm 127)

1. The first part of the psalm, verses 1–2, seems at first to be completely unrelated to the second part, verses 3–5, but as we will see, both parts actually fit together. As you consider the psalm as a whole, can you identify a theme or themes threading through the entire psalm?

UNLESS . . . (127:1–2)

These opening verses look a lot like the sayings we find in Proverbs, which isn't surprising, since Solomon, a prolific writer of proverbs, is the one who wrote this psalm. These verses show us how life is meant to be lived:

1 Unless the LORD builds the house,
those who build it labor in vain.

Unless the Lord watches over the city,
    the watchman stays awake in vain.
2 It is in vain that you rise up early
    and go late to rest,
eating the bread of anxious toil;
    for he gives to his beloved sleep. (127:1–2)

2. What do these verses teach us about work and labor?

3. What do these verses teach us about the Lord?

4. If you've ever struggled with insomnia, the inability to either fall asleep or stay asleep, perhaps you know firsthand that anxiety is at times a root cause. What does verse 2 reveal as the remedy?

5. Look again at the first part of verse 1: "Unless the Lord builds the house, those who build it labor in vain." A house is a dwelling, of course, but the term can also be used for "kingdom," similar to the way the word *dynasty* is often used. With that

in mind, Solomon might have been reflecting on God's promise to his father King David, a promise that was carried forward a generation later by Solomon himself. Read God's promise in 2 Samuel 7:1–16. In what way is that promise reflected here in the psalm?

FRUITFUL FAMILIES (127:3–5)

Verses 3–4 might seem completely unrelated to verses 1–2, but the word "house" in verse 1 actually ties them together. We've noted that *house* can be either a dwelling or a kingdom, but it can also mean "family," which comes into focus now:

> 3 Behold, children are a heritage from the LORD,
> the fruit of the womb a reward.
> 4 Like arrows in the hand of a warrior
> are the children of one's youth.
> 5 Blessed is the man
> who fills his quiver with them!
> He shall not be put to shame
> when he speaks with his enemies in the gate. (127:3–5)

The "reward" of children doesn't come from earning the Lord's blessings. Rather, it reflects a particular way—one of many—that the Lord blesses those who put their trust in him.

6. In what specific ways in verses 4–5 do children (sons in particular in this passage) serve as a "reward"?

7. How does the warrior imagery in these verses tie into the overarching theme of a "house" being built (keep in mind God's promise in 2 Samuel 7:1–16)?

8. We can see in the New Testament that the promises of Psalm 127 point beyond Solomon's time to a spiritual reality for God's people in our very own day. How do you see that in 1 Peter 2:4–5?

> *"It is profoundly true that only in dependence on God can we hope to achieve anything that lasts. This applies to our marriages and families, to the hopes for the birth of children, and to every project on any scale."*[26]

THE BIG PICTURE (PSALM 128)

Psalm 127 showed us the Lord's comprehensive care for his people and their complete dependence on him. Now, following directly from that, Psalm 128 shows us how to live in light of the Lord's care.

A Song of Ascents.

1 Blessed is everyone who fears the LORD,
who walks in his ways!
2 You shall eat the fruit of the labor of your hands;
you shall be blessed, and it shall be well with you.

3 Your wife will be like a fruitful vine
within your house;
your children will be like olive shoots
around your table.
4 Behold, thus shall the man be blessed
who fears the LORD.

5 The LORD bless you from Zion!
May you see the prosperity of Jerusalem
all the days of your life!
6 May you see your children's children!
Peace be upon Israel! (Psalm 128)

9. Underline repeated words and ideas in Psalm 128. Which words or ideas help you see the psalm's primary theme?

FRUITFUL FEAR (128:1–2)

The Bible's teaching about true wisdom is summed up clearly in the opening verses of Psalm 128:

1 Blessed is everyone who fears the Lord,
who walks in his ways!
2 You shall eat the fruit of the labor of your hands;
you shall be blessed, and it shall be well with you. (128:1–2)

10. The Bible's Wisdom Books link wisdom to the fear of the Lord (see, for example, Proverbs 9:10). This kind of fear isn't about being afraid of God. It's about orienting every aspect of our lives—all our plans and loves and choices—around him. So we're told here in the opening verses of Psalm 128 that wisdom is to fear the Lord and walk in his ways. What do you think it means to *walk* in the Lord's ways?

"God must be taken seriously. He must not be trifled with. He must be, as he actually is, the center of everything we are, think, or aspire to do. He must be our starting point for every project, the strength we seek for every valuable endeavor, the one we earnestly desire to please and honor as our goal."[27]

11. The language Solomon uses in these verses is "covenantal," which means it reflects God's promises of faithfulness to those who worship and serve him. While not a guarantee, what blessings does the psalm indicate generally come to those who orient their lives around the Lord?

A HAPPY HOME (128:3–4)

The psalmist's description of blessings broadens out from one faithful person to include his entire family:

> 3 Your wife will be like a fruitful vine
> within your house;
> your children will be like olive shoots
> around your table.
> 4 Behold, thus shall the man be blessed
> who fears the LORD. (128:3–4)

12. A godly man's wife and children will reap the rewards of his godly leadership. The vine and the olive in the Old Testament are symbolic of particular blessings. What impression do you get about both wife and children from the way these images are used here?

    - Wife like a fruitful vine:

    - Children like olive shoots:

BLESSINGS, BLESSINGS, AND MORE BLESSINGS (128:5–6)

Now the psalm broadens out even further to include future generations and all God's people:

> 5 The LORD bless you from Zion!
> May you see the prosperity of Jerusalem
> all the days of your life!
> 6 May you see your children's children!
> Peace be upon Israel! (128:5–6)

The psalm shows us that a godly individual is blessed, and a godly individual in turn blesses his family, and godly families strengthen and build up God's people as a whole.

13. None of us lives in the fear of the Lord perfectly or walks in all his ways. We know that we sin every day. Because that's true, we might find ourselves anxious as we study this psalm and wondering if our sins disqualify us and our families and friends from the blessings held out here. But Psalm 28 is merely a foretaste of even greater blessings in store for God's people. How are those blessings shown in Ephesians 1:3–10, and how do God's people receive them?

Festival Fact

In the Bible, yeast represents growth. "Often it is connected with the growth of evil or the spread of sin. This was its symbolic meaning during the Feast of Unleavened Bread. Whenever the Israelites celebrated this feast, they swept all the yeast out of their presence. "This was supposed to symbolize holiness. God's people were making a clean sweep, getting rid of the old life of sin. We do the same thing when we come to Jesus Christ. Once we trust in him for salvation, we have to leave behind the old life of sin. The Feast of Unleavened Bread gives us a picture of what it means to be sanctified in Christ."[28]

"Whether or not we are given to enjoy these literal blessings in this age, Psalm 128 sets before us supremely the blessings that are ours in Christ."[29]

LET'S TALK

1. Our labors, even the mundane chores we do on a daily basis, have meaning and bear spiritual fruit when they are done in dependence on the Lord. Describe a necessary task or chore you dislike doing. How can knowing that God is at work behind the scenes to accomplish his purposes change your attitude about this task?

2. Israel's annual treks to Jerusalem for worship meant setting aside all their responsibilities back at home, sometimes for weeks at a time. Even so, they made the journey in obedience to God. Talk about why their willingness to leave home required trust in God's care. Discuss also an area of your life in which obedience to God might require you to set aside something important. What specifically will you have to entrust into God's care and keeping in order to move forward?

3. When Jesus came, he gave a fuller picture of the blessings shown in Psalm 128, the blessedness that comes to those who orient their lives around God. Read what Jesus said in Matthew 5:2–12 and discuss how living the way he describes there blesses us, our families, and our Christian friends.

WEEK 7

KNOCKED DOWN BUT NEVER DEFEATED

PSALM 129

Our natural response to mistreatment is typically anger. This hot emotion so easily rises up whenever our rights are violated or when we feel threatened. As God's daughters, however, we know that self-protective or retaliatory anger doesn't reflect the gentleness of our Savior. We want to be able to respond to mistreatment in a way that pleases God, and that's what we'll learn as we study Psalm 129. As Israel journeys toward Jerusalem, they reflect on dark times from their past, times and seasons when they experienced severe afflictions. Across their generations they were mistreated as slaves in Egypt, oppressed by enemy nations, and, from the very beginning, harassed by the powers of evil. Yet here they are, on their way to worship, singing to the Lord. That's because, for God's people, oppression and evil never get the last word. Victory was sure for Israel, and it is sure for Christians today. We find this assurance in our study of Psalm 129. We're also going to see the God-honoring way to think about people who seek to harm us and learn how to pray for them.

THE BIG PICTURE (PSALM 129)

A Song of Ascents.

1 "Greatly have they afflicted me from my youth"—
let Israel now say—

2 "Greatly have they afflicted me from my youth,
 yet they have not prevailed against me.
3 The plowers plowed upon my back;
 they made long their furrows."
4 The Lord is righteous;
 he has cut the cords of the wicked.
5 May all who hate Zion
 be put to shame and turned backward!
6 Let them be like the grass on the housetops,
 which withers before it grows up,
7 with which the reaper does not fill his hand
 nor the binder of sheaves his arms,
8 nor do those who pass by say,
 "The blessing of the Lord be upon you!
 We bless you in the name of the Lord!" (Psalm 129)

1. As you consider the psalm as a whole, what do you see that enables us to consider the psalmist's tone as victorious rather than defeated?

A LOOK BACK (vv. 1–3)

The psalmist begins with a reflection on Israel's history:

1 "Greatly have they afflicted me from my youth"—
 let Israel now say—
2 "Greatly have they afflicted me from my youth,
 yet they have not prevailed against me.
3 The plowers plowed upon my back;
 they made long their furrows." (vv. 1–3)

When he speaks in the first person, "me," he is speaking for God's people as a whole.

2. What do you infer about Israel's suffering from the images the psalmist uses to describe it in these opening verses?

If you read through the Old Testament, you'll see the numerous afflictions Israel experienced, from slavery in Egypt to relentless attacks by pagan nations as they settled in the land of Canaan, and later as they sought to defend their homeland. The afflictions aren't confined to just the Old Testament. Believers in the early church suffered ongoing persecution for their faith, and it continues up to the present day. None of this means God was caught off guard or that he failed to protect his people. It's all happened exactly as he said it would (for a recap, review the sidebar on page 41). from the very beginning, when he told the serpent, "I will put enmity between you and the woman, and between your offspring and her offspring; he shall bruise your head, and you shall bruise his heel" (Genesis 3:15). He was talking about the forces of evil in their determination to destroy God's people. Yet the power of evil is ultimately no match for the "offspring" of the woman in Genesis 3:15.

As the representative of God's people, Jesus Christ was afflicted more than anyone. The primary goal of every evil initiative—in the psalmist's day and in ours—has always been to obliterate Jesus, along with God's plan to redeem his people through him. This evil objective is what lies behind all the persecution believers have experienced throughout history.

3. What do we learn from the psalmist in these verses about how Israel's past persecution turned out?

4. Why, according to the following passages, can God's people be sure of the outcome that the psalmist notes in verse 2?

    - Romans 16:20

    - Hebrews 2:14–16

DELIVERANCE ACCOMPLISHED (v. 4)

Having reflected on the pain of the past, the psalmist gives praise for the defeat of evil enemies:

> The LORD is righteous;
> he has cut the cords of the wicked. (v. 4)

5. The evil that the wicked inflict is described as "cords." Think about the purpose cords serve, what they are used for. How does this help us understand the effects of evil and the intentions of wicked people?

6. What do we learn about the nature of the Lord's righteousness in verse 4?

A LOOK AHEAD (VV. 5–8)

After reflecting on the past, the psalmist looks to the future with a prayer:

> 5 May all who hate Zion
> be put to shame and turned backward!
> 6 Let them be like the grass on the housetops,
> which withers before it grows up,
> 7 with which the reaper does not fill his hand
> nor the binder of sheaves his arms,
> 8 nor do those who pass by say,
> "The blessing of the LORD be upon you!
> We bless you in the name of the LORD!" (vv. 5–8)

7. These requests for the Lord to defeat the wicked are called "imprecatory" prayers. An imprecation is a curse, a wish for destruction. Here, the psalmist uses farming imagery to colorfully illustrate his imprecatory petitions. How do these images help us see what the psalmist is asking in each verse?

   - v. 5

   - v. 6

- v. 7

- v. 8

8. We can grow our understanding of Psalm 129 by taking a look at Psalm 2 as well.
    - How does Psalm 2 help us understand why the writer of Psalm 129 isn't wrong to pray for the destruction of Israel's enemies?
    - Where do you see an indication of God's grace held out to the rebellious in Psalm 2?

Festival Fact

The New Testament describes Jesus as "'the firstfruits of those who have fallen asleep' (1 Cor. 15:20). This is a clear reference to the Feast of Harvest, which started when the first sheaf of grain was waved before God. That first sheaf of grain was part of the harvest, but it also held the promise of much more to come . . . The Old Testament Feast of Firstfruits helps us understand the gospel by giving us a picture of both the first and the final resurrection."[30]

LET'S TALK

1. The world, the flesh (our sin nature), and the devil conspire against us the way Israel's enemies conspired against them. We are confident that one day, these trials and troubles will no longer plague us, but in the meantime, we sometimes get a taste of those "long furrows" along our backs! Discuss how Psalm 129 can serve as an encouragement to persevere. You might also want to look together at 2 Corinthians 4:7–11, 16–18 and 1 Peter 4:12–14.

2. We know it's right to pray that evil won't succeed, but if we're honest, imprecatory prayers like the one we encounter in Psalm 129 can make us a bit uncomfortable. Talk about how we can pray for those who despise the Lord, in a way that honors Christ and upholds God's righteousness.

3. God turns every trial and tragedy suffered by his people into something good. Sometimes we experience this good in visible, tangible ways. Other times the good fruit that God brings from suffering is hidden from our view, and we will realize it only later. Talk about the way this is clarified for us in Romans 8:28–30.

WEEK 8

HOPE, HUMILITY, AND TRUE HAPPINESS

PSALMS 130–131

Humility is an underrated virtue in our day. In fact, many see it as weakness. But the psalms we're studying this week show us why humility is actually strength—as well as the root of joy, peace, and blessing. First, Psalm 130 shows us that humility is necessary for facing our sin, dealing with guilt, and experiencing God's forgiveness. Then in Psalm 131 we see why humility and trust go hand in hand. It takes humility to trust God because it means embracing life on his terms, not ours. It means giving up the right to control our own lives. Humility is an eye-opener. It enables us to see reality—reality about God and about ourselves. Humility is also the paradoxical pathway to happiness, to a contented life. As Israel journeyed toward the place of God's presence in Jerusalem, they prepared their hearts through these prayerful songs. And these songs are for us too, as we further our own journey of discipleship on the road to our eternal home in God's presence.

THE BIG PICTURE (PSALM 130)

A Song of Ascents.

1 Out of the depths I cry to you, O LORD!
2 O Lord, hear my voice!
Let your ears be attentive
to the voice of my pleas for mercy!

3 If you, O LORD, should mark iniquities,
O Lord, who could stand?

4 But with you there is forgiveness,
that you may be feared.

5 I wait for the LORD, my soul waits,
and in his word I hope;
6 my soul waits for the Lord
more than watchmen for the morning,
more than watchmen for the morning.

7 O Israel, hope in the LORD!
For with the LORD there is steadfast love,
and with him is plentiful redemption.
8 And he will redeem Israel
from all his iniquities. (Psalm 130)

1. Underline repeated words and phrases in Psalm 130. How does the repetition reveal the primary purpose of the psalm, its overarching theme?

OUT OF THE DEPTHS (130:1–2)

As the psalm begins, the psalmist is at a spiritual low point:

1 Out of the depths I cry to you, O LORD!
O Lord, hear my voice!
2 Let your ears be attentive
to the voice of my pleas for mercy! (130:1–2)

2. In Scripture, the "depths" or the "deep"—words associated with going down—are sometimes a poetic way of describing particular situations or conditions. What sort of circumstances do these words bring to your mind?

3. What does the psalmist desire here in Psalm 130:1–2?

THE ONLY REMEDY (130:3–4)

Now the reason for the psalmist's low spirits becomes very clear:

> 3 If you, O LORD, should mark iniquities,
> O Lord, who could stand?
> 4 But with you there is forgiveness,
> that you may be feared. (130:3–4)

4. What can we infer from verses 3–4 for why the psalmist's soul is troubled?

5. In what does the psalmist ground his appeal for God's forgiveness?

6. According to verse 4, what happens in the heart of someone who truly experiences God's forgiveness?

Penitential Psalms

The seven penitential psalms are Psalms 6, 32, 38, 51, 102, 130, and 143.

7. The psalmist lived centuries before Christ came to redeem sinners on the cross and reconcile them to God. Even so, he expresses great confidence in the Lord's forgiveness. How does his confidence point forward to what's revealed in Romans 3:21–26?

> *"Psalm 130:3–4 brings us face to face with our sinfulness in stark honesty and then helps us feel the wonder and amazement that should accompany forgiveness."*[31]

WATCHING AND WAITING (130:5–6)

The psalmist is no longer in the depths when we get to these verses. Here he is waiting:

> 5 I wait for the Lord, my soul waits,
> and in his word I hope;

6 my soul waits for the Lord
  more than watchmen for the morning,
  more than watchmen for the morning. (130:5–6)

8. We want to consider what exactly the psalmist is waiting for. He's confident that his sin has been forgiven, so we know that he isn't waiting for forgiveness As you consider the way that the psalmist expresses his heart here, what do you think he is waiting for? (You'll find a hint in another plea for forgiveness. Psalm 51:8–12 sheds light on what the psalmist is waiting for here in Psalm 130.)

If you're prone to sleepless nights, lying awake hour after hour alone in the dark, then likely you know how comforting it is when the morning sky begins to lighten. Tired though you might be, the sunrise brings an end to the isolation of a sleepless night. Guilt has a similar effect on us, holding us captive in spiritual darkness and making us feel cut off from the Lord. This gets at the way the psalmist speaks of "morning" in verse 6.

9. How does 1 John 1:5–9 show us our own way out of the dark of a spiritual night?

HOPE THAT NEVER DISAPPOINTS (130:7–8)

It seems that the psalmist's longing for morning light has been satisfied, as he now calls fellow believers to share in his newfound joy:

7 O Israel, hope in the LORD!
  For with the LORD there is steadfast love,

and with him is plentiful redemption.
8 And he will redeem Israel
from all his iniquities. (130:7–8)

10. What reasons does the psalmist give for his confident call to hope?

11. Read Ephesians 2:1–9. How does this passage, especially verse 4, show us what these final verses of Psalm 130 point toward?

THE BIG PICTURE (PSALM 131)

A Song of Ascents. Of David.

1 O Lord, my heart is not lifted up;
my eyes are not raised too high;
I do not occupy myself with things
too great and too marvelous for me.
2 But I have calmed and quieted my soul,
like a weaned child with its mother;
like a weaned child is my soul within me.
3 O Israel, hope in the Lord
from this time forth and forevermore. (Psalm 131)

12. As we consider the psalm as a whole, we get an idea of the psalmist's spiritual condition from the way he describes himself. What do you glean from what he says about:

- His heart:

- His mind:

- His soul or spirit:

PORTRAIT OF CONTENTMENT (131:1)

This psalm from King David is written as a prayer. He begins by declaring his attitude and outlook:

> O Lord, my heart is not lifted up;
>   my eyes are not raised too high;
> I do not occupy myself with things
>   too great and too marvelous for me. (131:1)

13. In God's word, a lifted-up heart is a proud heart. David is saying that he isn't dominated by pride. What particular traits of pride does he seem to renounce in verses 1–2?

14. The opposite of a lifted-up heart, one that is proud, is a humble heart. Identify particular traits of humility by completing the Traits of a Humble Heart chart below.

Traits of a Humble Heart

	Traits Observed
Deuteronomy 8:2–3	
Psalm 149:4	
Proverbs 11:12	
Micah 6:8	
James 4:4–10	
1 Peter 5:6–7	

15. "Things too great and too marvelous" (v. 1) concern matters in which humans have limited knowledge or understanding. God in his wisdom doesn't reveal everything to us, but we can be confident that he has revealed all we need to know. What do you think underlies the temptation to obsess about unknowable things?

16. Despite King David's declaration of humility in verses 1–2, the Bible tells us of times when he didn't live this way! Surely, like all of us, he was tempted toward pride throughout his life. For that reason, we know that his declaration here points beyond David himself to the greater King, Jesus Christ, the only one who lived humbly all his days. How is Jesus's humility shown in Philippians 2:5–8?

Festival Fact

"We no longer celebrate the pilgrim feasts . . . There is a still a place for feasting, of course, and for celebrating salvation in Jesus Christ. But as Christians we are not required to go to Jerusalem three times a year for the Feasts of Unleavened Bread, Harvest, and Ingathering. These three feasts . . . all found their fulfillment in the saving work of Jesus Christ."[32]

CALM AND QUIET (131:2)

David uses a metaphor, the word-picture of a weaned child, to convey why he is humble and what keeps him that way:

> But I have calmed and quieted my soul,
> like a weaned child with its mother;
> like a weaned child is my soul within me. (131:2)

17. As you consider the psalm as a whole, what do you think it means to have a "calmed and quieted" soul?

HUMILITY'S GIFT (131:3)

David desires that all Israel would enjoy the spiritual riches of a humble heart, and as their leader, he calls them to share in his experience:

> O Israel, hope in the LORD
> from this time forth and forevermore. (131:3)

18. Why do you think that hope characterizes a heart that lives in submission to the Lord?

LET'S TALK

1. Do you long for or find yourself in need of restoration of intimacy with the Lord? Talk about how applying particular aspects of Psalm 130 can help you.

2. A humble heart is something God works in us as well as something we are called to cultivate in ourselves. Where can you detect God's humbling work in your life? Have you responded like David in Psalm 131? What fruit has your response produced in your life?

3. Talk about some traits that go hand in hand with humility: trust, contentment, and living for the Lord rather than ourselves. Which ones tend to be a struggle for you—and why?

WEEK 9

PROMISES KEPT

PSALM 132

I hope you love history, because in order to understand the meaning of the psalm we're studying this week, we have to look back at Israel's past. In the process, we're going to learn something important about God—he makes choices. God chooses particular people and places to accomplish his good purposes in the lives of all people in all places at all times. In Psalm 132 we see two such choices. God chose David as king, and he chose Jerusalem as the worship center for Israel and the city from which David would rule. These choices were confirmed when God made a covenant with David at the onset of his reign. As God's people made the trek to Jerusalem, they could sing Psalm 132 with celebratory gladness because they'd been swept up into the blessings God promised through his chosen king at his chosen place. Psalm 132 is called a "royal psalm" because it looks back on God's promises to David and, with confidence in God's faithfulness, prayerfully asks God to honor those promises. *A note before you begin: be sure to read the sidebar about the ark on page 95.*

THE BIG PICTURE (PSALM 132)

A Song of Ascents.

1 Remember, O LORD, in David's favor,
    all the hardships he endured,
2 how he swore to the LORD
    and vowed to the Mighty One of Jacob,
3 "I will not enter my house
    or get into my bed,

4 I will not give sleep to my eyes
  or slumber to my eyelids,
5 until I find a place for the Lord,
  a dwelling place for the Mighty One of Jacob."

6 Behold, we heard of it in Ephrathah;
  we found it in the fields of Jaar.
7 "Let us go to his dwelling place;
  let us worship at his footstool!"

8 Arise, O Lord, and go to your resting place,
  you and the ark of your might.
9 Let your priests be clothed with righteousness,
  and let your saints shout for joy.
10 For the sake of your servant David,
  do not turn away the face of your anointed one.

11 The Lord swore to David a sure oath
  from which he will not turn back:
"One of the sons of your body
  I will set on your throne.
12 If your sons keep my covenant
  and my testimonies that I shall teach them,
their sons also forever
  shall sit on your throne."

13 For the Lord has chosen Zion;
  he has desired it for his dwelling place:
14 "This is my resting place forever;
  here I will dwell, for I have desired it.
15 I will abundantly bless her provisions;
  I will satisfy her poor with bread.
16 Her priests I will clothe with salvation,
  and her saints will shout for joy.
17 There I will make a horn to sprout for David;
  I have prepared a lamp for my anointed.
18 His enemies I will clothe with shame,
  but on him his crown will shine." (Psalm 132)

1. Psalm 132 is referred to as a "royal" psalm. What words in the psalm convey the idea of royalty?

2. Read 2 Samuel 7:4–16, which recounts the covenant God made with David. Note how you see those covenant promises reflected here in Psalm 132.

The Ark of the Covenant

The ark was a wooden box about a yard long and eighteen inches high and deep covered with gold. It contained the law of God written on tablets of stone, and it was closed by a solid covering called the mercy seat, which was where the high priest sprinkled the blood of a sacrifice for the sins of the nation once a year on the Day of Atonement. The ark was made in the wilderness during the years of the people's wandering and was kept within the Most Holy Place of the portable wilderness tabernacle. It symbolized God's presence.[33]

DAVID'S DETERMINATION (vv. 1–5)

The psalmist prayerfully reflects on the time when King David determined to bring the ark to Jerusalem and to build a temple to house the ark. We want to keep in mind as we study these verses that the ark symbolized God's presence with his people.

> 1 Remember, O Lord, in David's favor,
> all the hardships he endured,

2 how he swore to the LORD
 and vowed to the Mighty One of Jacob,
3 "I will not enter my house
 or get into my bed,
4 I will not give sleep to my eyes
 or slumber to my eyelids,
5 until I find a place for the LORD,
 a dwelling place for the Mighty One of Jacob." (vv. 1–5)

David invested his kingly resources in getting the ark to Jerusalem and acquiring materials to build a temple. (Actual construction of the temple didn't happen until the reign of David's son Solomon.) The process of bringing up the ark included some setbacks along the way, but the mission was ultimately successful. (You can review the backstory in 2 Samuel 6:1–15.)

3. Scripture makes clear that God never forgets facts and details and people. So what do you think the psalmist means when he calls on God to "remember" his covenant promises to David in verse 1?

4. As king of Israel, David was responsible to oversee the nation's well-being—no light task! How do verses 1–5 reveal what ruled his heart and governed his priorities?

LOST AND FOUND (vv. 6–7)

As God's people make the ascent to Jerusalem to worship, they reflect on the ascent of the ark all those years ago:

> 6 Behold, we heard of it in Ephrathah;
> we found it in the fields of Jaar.
> 7 "Let us go to his dwelling place;
> let us worship at his footstool!" (vv. 6–7)

Long before David was king, Israel was defeated in battle by the enemy Philistines, who captured the ark. The Philistines' victory didn't last long, however, because the Lord brought trouble and sickness on them wherever they placed the ark. After seven months of these difficulties, the Philistines had had enough, and they sent the ark back to a place in Israel called Kiriath-jearim (called "Jaar" here in the psalm), where it remained until David brought it up to Jerusalem. During those intervening years, David's predecessor Saul was king, and the ark was all but forgotten by God's people. (It's a fascinating story of the Lord's power, and you can review it in 1 Samuel 5:1–7:2.)

5. How would you classify the mood of the travelers as they near the great city?

6. The Israelites persevered on their journey until they reached Jerusalem, the place of worship. In other words, they made an effort to get there. How does verse 7 reveal what motivated their efforts?

THE ANOINTED ONE (vv. 8–10)

The "anointed one" in verse 10 is most likely an Israelite king who came to the throne long after David and is accompanying the people to Jerusalem:

> 8 Arise, O Lord, and go to your resting place,
> you and the ark of your might.

9 Let your priests be clothed with righteousness,
and let your saints shout for joy.
10 For the sake of your servant David,
do not turn away the face of your anointed one. (vv. 8–10)

7. On what does this "anointed one" base his appeal for God's favor?

8. David is held up as the great king here, but all Israel knew that he'd made some really bad blunders as king and committed horrendous sins during his reign (see 2 Samuel 11–12). In light of this, it's logical to wonder why they were able to sing this psalm with such confidence. The reason is that the psalm, guided by the Holy Spirit, was composed to foreshadow a greater David, an "anointed one" who would rule God's people perfectly. How does Hebrews 1:8–9 identify this "anointed one"?

The reason for the joy seen here will make sense to us once we complete our history lesson. During the years when Israel wandered in the wilderness led by Moses, God's presence with them was symbolized by a cloud that rested over the tent or tabernacle that housed the ark. (This is summarized in Exodus 40:34–38.) When the cloud lifted, it was a sign to Israel that they were to pack up the tabernacle and all their belongings and trek onward until the cloud over the ark stopped moving. Each time the ark set out, Moses would say, "Arise, O Lord" (Numbers 10:35). This history is reflected here in Psalm 132:8. Years later in David's day, when the ark finally arrived at its permanent home in Jerusalem, there was a huge celebration. You'll find a record of that festive occasion in 2 Samuel 6:12–19, where King David and God's people rejoiced. All this history underlies Psalm 132.

9. What blessings do those singing Psalm 132 on their way to Jerusalem share in common with the travelers back in Moses's day and the joyful people in David's day?

10. At this point in our lesson, summarize why the ark was such a huge deal.

THE FOREVER KING (vv. 11–12)

These next verses point to one of the most important happenings in God's overarching plan to redeem his people:

> 11 The Lord swore to David a sure oath
>   from which he will not turn back:
> "One of the sons of your body
>   I will set on your throne.
> 12 If your sons keep my covenant
> and my testimonies that I shall teach them,
>   their sons also forever
>   shall sit on your throne." (vv. 11–12)

11. In what way is verse 11 a response, a counterpart, to verse 2 earlier in the psalm?

12. At the beginning of this lesson, you looked at the establishment of God's covenant with David in 2 Samuel 7:4–16. What specific promises from the covenant are celebrated here in Psalm 132:11–12?

God's promise in verse 12 presents a dilemma. We're told that God won't ever turn back from his promise to David, but it's conditioned on Israel's obedience: "*If* your sons keep my covenant . . ." The problem is, Israel failed to obey. So, because God never fails even when his people do, he provided a way—the only way—out of this dilemma. The remedy was planned from the beginning, but it was revealed in all its fullness much later, when the angel Gabriel announced to a frightened girl named Mary,

> Behold, you will conceive in your womb and bear a son, and you shall call his name Jesus. He will be great and will be called the Son of the Most High. And the Lord God will give to him the throne of his father David, and he will reign over the house of Jacob forever, and of his kingdom there will be no end. (Luke 1:31–33)

Festival Fact

The exodus from Egypt was remembered in the seven-day Feast of Unleavened Bread, which began with the Passover observance, slaying a lamb, smearing its blood on homes, and then roasting and eating the lamb. In this way God's people remembered how God freed them from slavery in Egypt, passing over Israelite houses when he struck down the firstborns of the Egyptians, because Israelite homes had been marked with the blood of a slain lamb. The night before he was crucified, Jesus established the feast of the Lord's Supper, on the Passover, to show that he was the one whom those slain lambs foreshadowed. "Just as the first exodus was preceded by the institution of the Passover, the greater new exodus was preceded by the institution of the Lord's Supper. Jesus instituted the Lord's Supper on this night to signify that this new exodus was about to begin. This act indicated that the time of redemption had come."[34]

ABUNDANT SATISFACTION (vv. 13–18)

Now the travelers rejoice in all the Lord has promised his people through his covenant with David:

> 13 For the LORD has chosen Zion;
> he has desired it for his dwelling place:
> 14 "This is my resting place forever;
> here I will dwell, for I have desired it.
> 15 I will abundantly bless her provisions;
> I will satisfy her poor with bread.
> 16 Her priests I will clothe with salvation,
> and her saints will shout for joy.
> 17 There I will make a horn to sprout for David;
> I have prepared a lamp for my anointed.
> 18 His enemies I will clothe with shame,
> but on him his crown will shine." (vv. 13–18)

13. These verses are God's answer to the prayer lifted up in verses 8–10. Note God's answer to each petition in the Covenant Promises chart below.

Covenant Promises

Prayer Requests in vv. 8–10	God's Answer in vv. 13–18
"Arise, O LORD, and go to your resting place, you and the ark of your might." (v. 8)	
"Let your priests be clothed with righteousness, and let your saints shout for joy." (v. 9)	
"For the sake of your servant David, do not turn away the face of your anointed one." (v. 10)	

14. The Lord's answers to those prayer requests reach far beyond King David and the traveling worshipers in Israel. How is this revealed in Revelation 21:1–5?

LET'S TALK

1. We focused a lot on *covenant* this week. A covenant is weighty, binding agreement We make covenants at times in our own lives. Have you been part of a particular covenant? If so, talk about what makes it solemn. What promises does the covenant bind you to and how are you doing at keeping them? How do your challenges with covenant-keeping contrast with the covenant-keeping God?

2. This has been an intense lesson! What did you learn about the way God works in and through people to fulfill his plans and promises? Reflect together on the significance of the ark, God's covenant with David, and the place of Jerusalem in God's plans.

3. God's people found great joy in thinking about God's covenant promises to David because those promises were intended to bless them too. Those promises have all been fulfilled in Jesus now, so we have even more to sing about. Talk about what it means to have Jesus not only as your Savior but also as your king. How does Jesus as King encourage or convict you?

WEEK 10

BONDED AND BLESSED

PSALMS 133–134

Six weeks ... five weeks ... four weeks ... the long-anticipated vacation lies just ahead. The closer we get, the more our excitement grows, even as our impatience becomes harder to resist. If you know what that's like, you've had a small taste of how Israel surely felt as they neared the end of their journey to Jerusalem. What awaited them was something way better than the best beach or guided tour. They were coming to the place of God's presence and to worship him there. And just as one of the best parts of vacation is experiencing it with loved ones, Israel shared together in worship at Jerusalem. They were united in purpose. We wrap up our study this week with the final two Psalms of Ascents. Psalm 133 is all about the blessings of unity, blessings intended not only for Israel but for believers today too. Then in Psalm 134 we get an inside look at Israel's worship practices, and from this short little psalm we learn about the sort of worship that pleases God. As we study these psalms, we can't help but find ourselves caught up in Israel's joy and praise.

THE BIG PICTURE (PSALM 133)

A Song of Ascents. Of David.

1 Behold, how good and pleasant it is
    when brothers dwell in unity!
2 It is like the precious oil on the head,
    running down on the beard,
on the beard of Aaron,
    running down on the collar of his robes!

3 It is like the dew of Hermon,
which falls on the mountains of Zion!
For there the LORD has commanded the blessing,
life forevermore. (Psalm 133)

1. Unity is clearly the theme of the psalm. David uses two similes (comparisons that use the word *like* or *as*) to describe this theme. Certain elements in these comparisons might be unfamiliar to us, but we can still grasp the big picture. What do David's similes tell us about unity?

HOW GOOD IT IS! (133:1)

Anyone who has experienced the sort of unity described in this psalm can echo the strong declaration with which it begins:

> Behold, how good and pleasant it is
> when brothers dwell in unity! (v. 1)

The first word, "Behold," calls us to take special note, to pay close attention to what follows. And as we do, we want to note that it's right to understand "brothers" as meaning all God's people—brothers and sisters, young and old.

2. Given the context of the psalm—its inclusion among the Psalms of Ascents—we can infer that when David describes the experience of God's people who "dwell" together, it means something more than living together under one roof. What do you think is meant by "dwell" here in verse 1?

3. Israel experienced the goodness of unity when they reached Jerusalem to worship and celebrate the annual feasts. Why do you think "good and pleasant" is a fit way to describe the fruit of unity?

LIKE PRECIOUS OIL (133:2)

Now we come to the first of David's comparisons—his first simile—about unity:

> It is like the precious oil on the head,
> running down on the beard,
> on the beard of Aaron,
> running down on the collar of his robes! (133:2)

In our day and age, it's hard to think past the lengthy cleanup from oil being poured on one's head and clothes, but in Israel it symbolized great blessing. Back in Israel's early days, Moses's brother Aaron and his descendants were set apart by God to serve as priests. They were consecrated for this service by anointing with a very special oil (Exodus 30:22–32). The role of the priests was to offer sacrifices for the sins of God's people, most importantly on the Day of Atonement, when the high priest carried out the sacrificial duties in the innermost part of the tabernacle, called the "Most Holy Place." Through the priest's service, guilt was cleansed, sin was paid for, and the people were reconciled to God. You might be wondering why David uses the priest Aaron's anointing to illustrate the blessings of unity. Here's why: "The anointing of Aaron was a blessing from God for him, but he was the high priest, which meant that he in turn blessed others. . . . The anointing would have been wonderfully fragrant and would have filled the air wherever Aaron went."[35]

4. Now that you know a bit about Aaron and the Old Testament priesthood, why do you think oil on Aaron's head is a good picture of what unity produces?

5. The link between unity and Aaron's anointing becomes even clearer when we understand that Aaron's priesthood pointed forward in time to Jesus's priesthood. Jesus is the Great High Priest, which we see most clearly in the New Testament letter to the Hebrews. A good portion of that letter is devoted to showing us Christ in his priestly role. How is Christian unity portrayed for believers living under Christ's priesthood in Hebrews 10:19–25?

LIKE THE DEW OF HERMON (133:3)

In David's second comparison, he says that unity is like dew:

> It is like the dew of Hermon,
> which falls on the mountains of Zion!
> For there the LORD has commanded the blessing,
> life forevermore. (133:3)

Mount Hermon was the highest mountain in Israel, and apparently it was known for its well-watered peak. Dew in the Old Testament was a sign of God's favor (you'll find examples in Hosea 14:5 and Zechariah 8:11–12).

6. What fruit of unity can you see in David's picture of dew in verse 3?

7. The message here is that joyful fellowship is a gift that comes when people are united in their purpose. As you consider when these Psalms of Ascents were most likely sung (while traveling to Jerusalem), what primary purpose united God's people on those occasions?

THE BIG PICTURE (PSALM 134)

A Song of Ascents.

1 Come, bless the Lord, all you servants of the Lord,
who stand by night in the house of the Lord!
2 Lift up your hands to the holy place
and bless the Lord!
3 May the Lord bless you from Zion,
he who made heaven and earth! (Psalm 134)

8. It seems that the travelers have reached their destination. They have made it to Jerusalem. What do you see in the psalm that indicates this?

HERE AT LAST! (134:1–2)

Here is the whole reason for the journey to Jerusalem:

1 Come, bless the Lord, all you servants of the Lord,
who stand by night in the house of the Lord!
2 Lift up your hands to the holy place
and bless the Lord! (134:1–2)

Verses 1–2 address the temple personnel, the priests and the worship leaders, some of whom were called to serve in the temple day and night (this is noted in 1 Chronicles 9:33).

9. How do these verses show Israel's *attitude* toward worship?

10. What do these verses indicate about Israel's *focus* in worship?

11. All God's people were to bless the Lord in worship, but in view especially here are those who lead the people through it. What do these verses tell us about what characterizes godly ministers?

BLESS YOU! (134:3)

The final verse in this final Psalm of Ascents is a blessing on God's people:

> May the LORD bless you from Zion,
> he who made heaven and earth! (134:3)

12. How does the psalmist describe the Lord in verse 3, and what significance do you think this description adds to his closing blessing?

Festival Fact

"Salvation is worth celebrating, as we've seen all through our study of these psalms. But it doesn't end here. In fact, as we near the very end of the Bible, we're told about a feast yet to come, the marriage supper of the Lamb. This banquet . . . celebrates not only the final defeat of the enemies of Christ but also the marriage of the Lamb to a bride whom He has made worthy of her husband. Adorned in fine white linen, the church is united to Christ in a glorious celebration (Rev. 19:7–8)."[36]

13. Zion—Jerusalem—was the designated place of worship for Israel. All that changed when Christ came. Christian believers, those united to Christ by faith, have God's presence indwelling their very being by means of the Holy Spirit, so they can worship the Lord everywhere. According to the following passages, how does the Lord bless believers today as they gather for worship?

- 1 Corinthians 12:4–7

- Hebrews 10:23–25

14. How does Revelation 21:1–4 show us how Psalm 134 will ultimately be fulfilled?

LET'S TALK

1. We learned this week that the Lord values unity among his people and delights to bless it. Look together at Ephesians 4:1–7, 11–16 and note the blessings of unity you see there. How are these blessings visible in your faith community? Talk about how you contribute to that unity and also profit from it.

2. Talk about what you learned from this week's lesson about the sort of worship that pleases God.

3. As we come to the end of the Psalms of Ascents, note what you've learned or what's affected you most about:

   - the character of God:

   - the gospel of salvation through Jesus Christ:

   - the path of discipleship:

HELPFUL RESOURCES FOR STUDYING THE PSALMS OF ASCENTS

Ash, Christopher. *The Psalms: A Christ-Centered Commentary*. 4 vols. Wheaton, IL: Crossway, 2024.

Boice, James Montgomery. *Psalms: An Expositional Commentary*. 4 vols. Grand Rapids, MI: Baker, 1998.

Kidner, Derek. *Psalms 73–150*, Tyndale Old Testament Commentaries. Edited by D. J. Wiseman. Downers Grove, IL: InterVarsity Press, 1973.

Waltke, Bruce K., and Fred G. Zaspel. *How to Read and Understand the Psalms*. Wheaton, IL: Crossway, 2023.

NOTES

1. "Jerusalem in the Time of Solomon," map from page 670–71 of the ESV® Study Bible (The Holy Bible, English Standard Version®), © 2008 by Crossway, a publishing ministry of Good News Publishers. Used by permission. All rights reserved.
2. Augustine, cited in Christopher Ash, *The Psalms: A Christ-Centered Commentary*, 4 vols. (Crossway, 2024), 4:330.
3. ESV® Study Bible (Crossway, 2008), note on 1 Kings 19:5.
4. Philip Graham Ryken, *Exodus*, Preaching the Word, ed. R. Kent Hughes (Wheaton, IL: Crossway, 2005), 758.
5. Bruce K. Waltke and Fred G. Zaspel, *How to Read and Understand the Psalms* (Crossway, 2023), 150.
6. Waltke and Zaspel, *How to Read and Understand the Psalms*, 152.
7. Waltke and Zaspel, *How to Read and Understand the Psalms*, 152.
8. Waltke and Zaspel, *How to Read and Understand the Psalms*, 151.
9. Waltke and Zaspel, *How to Read and Understand the Psalms*, 151.
10. Ryken, *Exodus*, 756.
11. *The Wizard of Oz*, directed by Victor Fleming and King Vidor (1939).
12. James Montgomery Boice, *Psalms: An Expositional Commentary*, 4 vols. (Baker, 1998), 3:1082–83.
13. Boice, *Psalms*, 3:1084.
14. "Jerusalem in the Time of Hezekiah," illustration from page 890–91 of the ESV® Study Bible (The Holy Bible, English Standard Version®), © 2008 by Crossway, a publishing ministry of Good News Publishers. Used by permission. All rights reserved.
15. Boice, *Psalms*, 3:1085.
16. Ryken, *Exodus*, 756–57.
17. Boice, *Psalms*, 3:1088.
18. *Merriam-Webster*, s.v. "despise," https://www.merriam-webster.com.
19. Boice, *Psalms*, 3:1101.
20. Ryken, *Exodus*, 757.

21. Boice, *Psalms*, 3:1107.
22. Christopher Ash, *The Psalms: A Christ-Centered Commentary*, 4 vols. (Crossway, 2024), 4:388.
23. Derek Kidner, *Psalms 73–150*, Tyndale Old Testament Commentaries, ed. D. J. Wiseman (InterVarsity Press, 1973), 439n3.
24. Ryken, *Exodus*, 757.
25. Philip Eveson, cited in Ash, *The Psalms*, 4:391.
26. Ash, *The Psalms*, 4:407.
27. Boice, *Psalms*, 3:1125.
28. Ryken, *Exodus*, 759.
29. Ash, *The Psalms*, 4:417.
30. Ryken, *Exodus*, 759.
31. Ash, *The Psalms*, 4:439.
32. Ryken, *Exodus*, 761.
33. Boice, *Psalms*, 3:1153.
34. Keith Mathison, "Why Did Jesus Institute the Lord's Supper on the Passover?," Ligonier, April 23, 2024, https://www.ligonier.org/.
35. Boice, *Psalms*, 3:1160.
36. "The Marriage Supper of the Lamb," Ligonier, December 11, 2020, https://www.ligonier.org/.

Flourish Bible Study Series

Judges

Esther

Job

The Psalms of Ascents

Ecclesiastes

Jonah

Habakkuk

Luke

Romans

Ephesians

Philippians

Colossians

James

1–2 Peter